PROJECT FAB!

NO MORE MAKING DO

Your guide to confidence with colour & clothes

LISA NEWPORT

First printing: 2021

ISBN-13: 978-1-3999-0388-2

Published by Lisa Newport Publishing

British Cataloguing Publication Data: A catalogue record of this book is available from The British Library.

Also available for Kindle from Amazon.

Dedication

In memory of my mum, my best and most loyal friend,
the lovely, generous and feisty Christine Newport.
Always beautifully turned out and an inspiration.
She NEVER made do.

Contents

Foreword

Having worked in the image consulting industry for many years, it still surprises me that people think I work exclusively with wealthy "ladies that lunch", that what I do is fluffy or vacuous, or that it's based purely on analysing the colours that suit you.

All the above might have been true at one time.

That was then. This is now.

I saw my first image consultant when I was working for a large corporate back in the early 1990s, when image consulting was pretty much a new concept. What I learned jump-started my trajectory from the low end of the rungs to the top end of the career ladder. I had no idea that just changing what I wore could have such a major effect. Unlikely as it might seem, when you change your clothes, you really can change your life.

It's a fact that we all need to wear clothes and choosing what to wear can be a joyful experience. It can also be frustrating, stressful and confidence-denting. Today we have WFH, Zoom calls and the demise of the corporate suit, older women wanting to look amazing, young people desperate to look good for an interview, dating, fast fashion versus sustainable ethical clothing, and advice for shopping in your own wardrobe. These are just a few reasons why the service we offer is extremely valuable.

You may remember the television makeover series and accompanying books, *What Not To Wear*. It was highly successful and led to similar shows such as *10 Years Younger* and *How To Look Good Naked*. While the transformations might have been spectacular, they were probably not long term. Most of the change was on the outside, not on the inside. And that's the rub!

A successful wardrobe depends entirely on WHO you are at your very core. The essential you when everything else is stripped away. Once you've nailed that, any changes that come about because of your appearance, lifestyle, relationships or intentions can be easily modified to suit. Rather than *What Not To Wear*, maybe *We Are What We Wear* would be more apt?

Whether or not you're aware of it, your clothes form a strategic part of your "wellness" toolbox. When you feel good, you look good – and you have less stress as a result. Your internal and external personas are aligned. You become more comfortable and confident. Because you are more self-assured, you attract what you want in your life and in your relationships. That's the power of clothes!

If you're unsure what I mean, think about a time you wore something unsuitable for a particular occasion, or your too-tight skirt kept riding up your thighs every time you sat down. Or envisage how you would feel if you accidentally splashed coffee onto your shirt when you're about to meet someone important. Uncomfortable attire not only plays on your mind, it shows up on your face.

An image consultation is never solely about clothing. A good consultant will enable you to discover who you are, where you are going and how to dress for it. It's a cliché, I know, but it really is a journey. One that will continue to inspire and inform as you go through life.

Lisa and I met a few years ago via a mutual colleague. We gelled immediately because of our like-minded views on helping clients find their own authentic style. We both favour a collaborative approach where clients "own" what they discover, rather than the didactic "rules" that can prevent you from wearing something you might love.

I admire Lisa because she is approachable, creative, ethical, honest, warm and highly professional. She's appeared on TV and has an impressive educational background. Lisa does this work because it calls to her. It's her vocation, her passion. Every client knows instinctively that she has their best interests at heart. That's the kind of person you need when your personal style – a very intimate aspect of your being – is the centre of attention.

Please be aware that there are many people who have no idea what suits them – and that's okay. There is no shame in this. Not everyone has the skill to put outfits together, just like not everyone can cook cordor bleu meals. If you find you are one of the multitudes that has a wardrobe of clothes and nothing to wear, or you struggle to find clothes that suit you, then you are in the right place. Lisa's book will help you to dress so you always feel like the best version of yourself, regardless of occasion, shape, culture or lifestyle. Her book is an extension of her face-to-face approach, so you are in good hands.

When you open the pages, you are entering the world of friendship, wisdom and nurturing. Lisa has been there, done it and got the proverbial t-shirt. Sharing personal stories of restricting dress codes, body dysmorphia, her low points and her highs, you'll see immediately that she most definitely "walks the talk". Using helpful tips or more insightful projects, you can skim the surface or delve deep, depending on what you need. She acts as your guide, coach and best friend, never judging, always encouraging.

This is the type of book you can dip into time and time again. Life never stands still, so expect the way you dress to also evolve. Finding your style isn't a once in a lifetime task, but something that changes as you change. Think of this book as an investment. An investment in the most important person in your life – YOU!

Sue Donnelly AICI CIP, LFIPI, FFSM
Mindful Dresser

Sue Donnelly AICI CIP, FFSM, LFIPI is an international award-winning image professional and a previous holder of the AICI Jane Segerstrom Award. Her mantras include "one size does not fit all" and "life evolves, style evolves".

She is a Past President, Fellow and Masters Award Assessor of the UK image industry's governing body, Federation of Image Professionals

International, a founding member of Association of Stylists and Image Professionals, a Certified Image Professional AICI (Association of Image Professionals International) and the Lead Trainer, and the only Master, of Fashion Feng Shui® in the UK. She is currently serving as VP Education for AICI (Association of Image Consultants International).

Sue is a certified coach, facilitator, author of five books, and regular style expert in magazines and on TV. She has been a sought-after speaker at conferences, presenting her unique slant on image-related topics all over the world. Your image tells your story, so it makes sense to choose what you want to say (albeit non-verbally) to convey personality, passion, principles and purpose. She believes that mindfully choosing what to wear is empowering, liberating and crucial to the enhancement of physical and mental well-being.

Who Is This Book Not For?

'The way we dress affects the way we think, the way we act, and the way others react to us.'

Judith Rasband

I tend to find that, generally, there are three types of women when it comes to personal style and image confidence.

1. Those who are innately stylish, would look good in a bin bag and are always perfectly turned out.
2. Those who are not that interested in how they look. If things are clean and comfortable, they're good.
3. Those who like to look nice and enjoy taking care with their appearance but aren't always 100% sure they're getting it right.

Type 1 already has personal style and image confidence. You do not NEED my services. This book has not been written for you.

Type 2 already has personal style and image confidence too, albeit in a different way to Type 1. You do not WANT my services. This book has not been written for you either.

Type 3 is the kind of woman who my work resonates with. You like to LOOK GOOD and FEEL FAB in your clothes. The problem is you have a wardrobe full of stuff but still feel like you've got nothing to wear, and this makes you frustrated (and more). This book has been written for you.

If you're Type 3, then you're in the right place... Let me take you on a journey and guide you through the principles of my Project FAB! framework.

Who Is This Book For?

'Be yourself; everyone else is already taken.'

Oscar Wilde

If you're anything like me, you want that feeling of confidence, when you look good and feel fab in your clothes. You've got to the stage where you think life is too short to feel miserable every time you look in the mirror. You know who you are and you want to show it, expressing yourself through the way you dress.

You want to look on trend but then start worrying about looking like mutton dressed as lamb.

You are definitely NOT ready for a twinset and pearls or wearing those Velcro-fastening shoes from the back of the Sunday supplements. Neither do you want to dress like your daughter.

You are somewhere in the middle: young at heart and want to look nice but aren't always sure that you've got your outfit 100% right. It doesn't seem that easy to get things feeling perfect, so you walk out of the door feeling self-assured.

There was a time when I felt quite overwhelmed when it came to putting an outfit together to go for a night out with friends. I had a wardrobe full of clothes, but I was practically wailing in my head, 'I've got nothing to wear!' How was it possible to have a wardrobe crammed full yet have NOTHING to wear? It didn't make sense.

I'm an intelligent, educated woman in the prime of her life. I was in a well-paid job with lots of responsibility. Yet, standing in my own bedroom and faced with my own possessions, I remember feeling so inadequate. This should be easy, surely?

For many women, these feelings are kept hidden even from close friends (and certainly from colleagues) because it makes them feel a bit stupid and silly. Inferior, even. I know this because it's how I felt, and clients tell me so too.

It's a guilty secret – I mean, shouldn't we all know how to dress ourselves, FFS?

The truth is I was suffering from wardrobe incompetence and had WTF* Syndrome (*Wardrobe That's Failing). My wardrobe wasn't on my side; I'd bred a monster.

If you're like I was back then, you probably have lots of *clothes* but struggle with *outfits*. There's a difference.

That's why you have a wardrobe full of clothes and still feel like you've got nothing to wear. You might feel frustrated and get cross with yourself. Then you go shopping, on the hunt for those "unicorn" items that are going to solve all your wardrobe woes – and you repeat the same patterns. The item feels good the first time you wear it, then ends up at the back of the wardrobe, adding to the growing pile that leaves you feeling bad about yourself.

If this sounds like you then you'll be pleased to know you're in good company. I hear this kind of story often. It's the kind of woman I used to be until I learned that you could hone the language of colour and clothes.

I created my business because I remember how frustrating it was to sit amongst a pile of clothes, close to tears and not wanting to go out with friends because I felt awful. I also believe that you deserve to and can look good and feel fab regardless of your age or body shape. I understand that you don't have loads of time to faff about every day, which is why I designed my four step Project FAB! framework to help women like you create a style recipe that makes choosing and buying clothes to create gorgeous outfits not only easier but fun too.

I understand you want to get out of the rut you've found yourself in, start to have fun with your clothes and enjoy your wardrobe.

This book is about elevating your personal style and image, so you feel empowered to dress with confidence. It's more about self-expression and identity using colour and clothes to convey who you are than following fashion trends and who wore what at the Oscars – that's just not my area of interest.

My area of expertise is about empowering you to invest time and energy into understanding yourself and what you want your clothes to say about you. It will mean having a word with yourself and recognising that you need to invest in the relationship with yours truly. It is about no longer putting yourself and your needs at the bottom of the pile but acknowledging that your happiness is important, and it impacts every aspect of your life. It is about hearing when you say, 'That will do' and shouting back 'No it won't!'

Tackling your wardrobe and changing the relationship you have with clothes is a form of self-care and whilst it took me several years and some formal qualifications, I want to provide you with a shortcut to the joy of having confidence in your own personal style and image.

We all must wear clothes daily, so why not have them working with you rather than against you?

Imagine transforming your wardrobe from one that is failing to one that is supporting your well-being and serving you.

This is where understanding what works for you as an individual comes into its own. For that to happen, you need to feel comfortable and confident that you're expressing your identity authentically. When you know what you want your clothes to say about you, not only will you be happy in your own skin and feel like you have nailed your personal style, but you will also always know what to wear and get dressed without the stress.

Project FAB!

This book will help you to be your own project with a view to projecting FAB!

Project: a piece of research, carefully planned to achieve a particular aim. It also means to present or convey a particular image – which in this case is one of being fab!

Project FAB! is about making you and your image a priority and helping you do the research so you can carefully plan out what you need to feel wonderful in everything you wear and have that deep sense of knowing you are fab. It is about helping you become the flamingo amongst the flock of pigeons! Because **F**abulous **L**adies **A**lways **M**ake an **I**mpression and **N**ever **G**et **O**verlooked!

Look good, feel fab, then go conquer the world!

What to Expect from This Book

'A girl should be two things: who and what she wants.'

Coco Chanel

This book is not a magic wand that will change your world overnight because you've got it on your bookshelf. Just in the same way as signing up for a slimming club or the gym doesn't make you slimmer or fitter. You will need to take action and do the work.

Saying that, I know you are a busy woman so I've formatted this book with lots of subheadings so you can skim read and then go back to the bits you deem to be a priority.

To get the most from it you will need to read, digest and implement the information I'm providing. You need to recognise and acknowledge first and foremost that you are worth it, invest some time and make Project FAB! a priority by putting yourself at the front of the queue. Commit to no more making do.

I've designed this book so there are structured opportunities for you to reflect on and exercises to spur you into action. It's a joint project if you like – written by me and personalised by you. It's the kind of book I'd like to have had myself when I was surrounded by clothes and didn't know where to start. It's a hybrid book/workbook/journal with written tasks, a bit of cutting and sticking and colouring in thrown in too. This will help you reconnect with your creativity. Enjoy customising it.

There are three interchangeable levels for each task depending on how much depth you want to go into and how much time you want to invest. You can pick and mix as you choose.

– **Level F** – this is the foundation level of the task and won't take long to do. You may simply make notes in this book where indicated.

  If you're one of those people who doesn't like to mutilate books by writing in them or turning the corners over to save your place, then you could visit my website and download the PDF workbook.

  https://www.lisanewportstyle.com/project-fab-the-book/

– **Level A** – this level of task is more advanced and will need a bit more time and effort.

  You can make notes in this book but might need more space for the colouring, cutting and sticking so I highly recommend the workbook download option for you.

– **Level B** – this level of task is best practice if you are committed to making bigger changes.

  You can make notes in this book but will definitely need more space. The workbook will get you started. You might also enjoy treating yourself to a lovely pen and beautiful notebook to journal and reflect in as you complete the tasks. This journey will be worth tracking and you're worth it.

The tasks are not compulsory, obviously, but I know you will gain a deeper insight and elevate your personal style and image confidence to the next level if you treat it like an actual project and do your homework. You could always start at Level F and then upgrade later once you've consolidated your learning.

I've made it my job here to share some practical advice and tips with you. I've woven in some stories to explain how and why I personally made the shift from making do to personal style and image confidence and how many of my clients have done the same.

I've delivered the four step Project FAB! framework both online and in person at workshops and as part of my one to one and group coaching work with individuals since 2015 and I'm now sharing with you the underpinning principles I've used to guide every client through the process.

Think about your Project FAB! style journey as you evolve into a new version of you, an upgraded model. Still yourself, but a more vibrant version, with a glow and confidence that comes from the inside.

Working on your personal style and image confidence is not about quick fixes and big reveals. It's very much about sustainable transformation, ensuring that any changes are able to be lasting and fit with your lifestyle.

My ethos is very much aligned with the Chinese proverb 'Give a man a fish and you feed him for a day; teach a man to fish and you feed him for a lifetime.'

My Promise

'The joy of dressing is an art.'

John Galliano

The fact that you are reading this book shows that you are at least curious and motivated to make some changes. Once you make time to invest in your appearance and begin to implement the framework it will help stop you mindlessly rifling through your wardrobe, and the scattergun approach to clothes shopping. No more wasting money on things you won't wear and no more making do.

You'll have a clearer idea of what you like and why you like it and an insight into your personal style choices, so you buy fewer items yet can open your wardrobe and at once be able to choose clothes that are not only right for what you are doing that day, but make you look and feel amazing too!

It will help you find CLARITY around your personal style.

It will show you how to choose colours and clothes so that you HAVE FUN, feel COMFORTABLE and CONFIDENT and ENJOY your wardrobe.

By implementing my framework, you will be safe in the knowledge that you're EXPRESSING your IDENTITY, in clothes that suit your LIFESTYLE and, most of all, feel perfect for YOU.

Ditch the DOUBTS

Does This Sound Like You?

'Don't compromise yourself - you're all you have.'

John Grisham, The Rainmaker

Ok, we've already established you aren't ready to disappear into a middle-aged void of mediocrity, nor are you overjoyed by what looks back at you in the mirror. You sometimes stress about getting dressed.

You might see stuff you like in magazines but then aren't sure if you're too old to go in "those" shops, or how to incorporate the trendy stuff into your outfits without looking and feeling a bit daft.

Wardrobe Wobbles

You may be aware that you have some emotional baggage around clothes and confidence that is being carried around unnecessarily. Maybe there was a mean comment from a sibling, or something a nasty boy said at school, and here you are, 40+ years later, still not wearing a skirt because somebody once said you had knobbly knees or tree trunk legs. This is when it's great to journal and allow those subconscious thoughts to flow onto the page.

The little voices in your head can reinforce those messages, resulting in SID the self-image demon coming out to play, leaving you with what I lovingly call a wardrobe wobble.

Not to mention the fact that your body shape has probably changed, and you aren't entirely happy with it or sure what suits you anymore. Things might be a bit softer than they used to be, not as taut. You could be hot one minute, cold the next and possibly getting less tolerant of synthetic fabrics and tight-fitting waistbands.

Heels you used to love are for looking at or special occasion "car to bar" type nights out – which are few and far between. Whilst you're not ready for going out in your cosy sheepskin slippers, you absolutely want your feet to be comfy.

Knowing what used to work but doesn't anymore can result in wardrobe wobbles. I want to reassure you that these are normal and are to be embraced as part of your Project FAB! I cannot guarantee that you will never feel frustrated again, but I can assure you that over time you will learn about what works for you and eventually your wardrobe will be a joy to open and creating "your look" will be fun.

So, learn to take the wardrobe wobbles for what they are. They are moments of awareness that something is not working and an opportunity for you to delve deeper and find a solution.

Clothes Shopping

I suspect you're not that keen on clothes shopping these days – it's all a bit too much like hard work. You might be ordering online, if you're lucky enough that your size is in stock, only to be sorely disappointed when it arrives. Then there's the hassle of sending stuff back – free returns are always a deal clincher. And what about real-life shopping? Traipsing around, you can never find anything and feel disheartened – and don't even get started on the changing rooms and being all hot and bothered. And that's before the hot flushes kick in.

Then you might feel guilty about paying full price, so you restrict yourself to the sale rails or charity shops. This means because you didn't pay full price, you're more likely to make do. So you end up with lots of items in your wardrobe that aren't quite making your heart sing when you wear them but hey, they were a "bargain", so in your head it doesn't matter so much if they end up unworn at the back of the wardrobe. And there they stay, taking up space, despite the many attempts to find something to go with them – which end up being also not quite right. The charity shop loves it when you get around to having a clear out.

There is a section of supermarket purchases in the wardrobe too – panic buys from Sainsbury's for those nights out with the girls when it is someone's birthday. The "jeans and a nice top" nights where you go to a local bistro/bar and have tapas and a few cocktails. You know that these clothes aren't that green/eco-friendly/sustainable/ethical, so that's another guilt trip – but needs must.

Work

You might work in an environment where the dress code is fairly relaxed most of the time – here lies a problem because you struggle with how to dial things up a notch when you have a presentation to deliver or need to represent the department externally. You might even think to yourself, 'WTF does smart casual even mean??'

It could be that you have a "game face" that you must wear in your work environment. You need to be an authority, credible, confident, and well respected; you stress about getting dressed and not feeling nice in your clothes these days is impacting you more than you'd like to think.

Hair & Make-up

Perhaps your hair texture has changed, and the greys are getting harder to disguise; you're wondering if it's time to embrace it – after all, Helen Mirren and Meryl Streep look bloody amazing! You might've started getting it professionally coloured as the box dye you used to use started to look a bit flat, and up to now that's been your biggest "self-care" expense. You might feel a bit guilty about that too; you're so used to putting others' needs first it feels a bit alien to you.

The make-up you've always worn seems to be making your skin

look worse rather than better; it's sitting in the lines. You've bought a few different products to try but feel apprehensive about approaching the counters as the sales staff are either too "cakey" or too young. You may have recently started to think about eye cream and neck cream and are wondering if it's too late to start.

Resolving the Issues

The problem is you have been trying to resolve these issues with more shopping but it's not getting any better and you're driving yourself mad – because you keep making the same mistakes.

You're competent, self-assured and comfortable complaining if the food is not up to scratch when you go out for lunch with friends. You're strong, resilient and have the wisdom that you get from reaching your age. You want to enjoy being who you are and explore how you want to express yourself with your clothes. Life is short, you get that, and you want to have a bit more fun...

If this sounds like you then you'll be pleased to know you're not alone. I hear these kinds of stories all the time. (I've already admitted it used to be me.) You've got to a point in your life where you are fed up with putting yourself at the back of the queue.

Overall, you're sick of wearing the same old stuff and are in danger of feeling invisible. But you are not ready to blend into the background and still feel young at heart.

It's time to learn how to reflect what is on the inside with your appearance.

All you really want is to look nice and feel good in your clothes rather than it all being a bit trial and error. You're so done with wasting time and money and still not really being 100% certain whether it works for you. You want to KNOW for sure and DRESS WITH CONFIDENCE. To be able to DITCH THE DOUBT and clamber out of the rut you've found yourself in, acknowledging that you are ready to embrace Project FAB! and are no longer going to make do.

You may have a "thing" that has made you curious enough to read this book. It might be business related. You recognise that to step up in your career you need to be more visible, putting yourself out there on social media. Or it might be that your body shape has changed, or you've experienced a major life event like losing a parent, redundancy, workplace trauma or divorce, and you think life is too short to be frustrated by your clothes anymore.

It could simply be that you feel you deserve more "me time" and have decided to put yourself first for a change.

So... In Summary

You would like to look nice but haven't got the time or inclination to be one of those high maintenance, perfectly coiffed and made-up types. You're feeling in a rut, getting frustrated, having more wardrobe wobbles than wardrobe wins and just wishing it was all a bit EASIER.

Congratulations! It will be easier now you're finally becoming your own project and are no longer going to make do. #bemoreyou

The Good News

You've now got the book with the principles of my tried and tested framework, so now I'm inviting you to raise your standards as far as you're concerned – value yourself enough to make time to get your appearance sorted.

Once you feel secure in your personal style and image, genuinely expressing who you are on the inside, the result will be that you exude radiance and confidence... and then who knows what the ripple effect will be for you?

Be
more
YOU

Meet Lisa

'If I ever tell you about my past, it's not because I want you to feel sorry for me but so you can understand why I am who I am.'

Author unknown

Short on time and don't need details?

My Bio in 200 Words

Born 1964, Lancashire. Hip problems from birth; surgery, scars, self-conscious. Limp, bullied. School, A levels, make-up training. Bar work. Hip problems, more surgery, more scars. Thought I was fat. Wasn't fat. Degree in textiles and fashion design, Loughborough College of Art and Design. Thought I was fat. Wasn't fat. Nottingham, flat share with a drag queen. Designer. Part-time lecturer. Thought I was fat. Not fat. Diet. Less fat. Full-time lecturer, Dewsbury, 140-mile commute. More surgery. Thought I was fat. Not fat. RTA, hit by a lorry, whiplash, PTSD, depression. Got married. Another RTA, six car pile-up, whiplash, depression, counselling. Pregnant, five stone weight gain. Became fat. Became a mum. Very happy. Award-winning consultant with Virgin Cosmetics; met Sir Richard Branson. Lost identity. Still fat. Depression. Teacher at HMP Nottingham, found identity, promotion to education manager. Happy. Still fat. Hip replacement. Lost identity again. Depression. Making do. Divorce. No more making do. Flamingos, leopard print, pink, glitter, found identity x 10. Inner peace. Reiki, colour analysis and style training. Own business. Still fat but happy. Met soulmate. Even happier. Married. Became a step mum. Business growing. Loving life. Still fat. More me than ever. Helping others elevate their personal style and image confidence.

That's it. You're done. You've got the gist of who I am – now fast forward to page 29.

Got a bit more time and want a few details?

Meet Lisa – The 5-minute Version

If you'd met me 10 or so years ago, I'd have been wearing a black leather belt. Attached to that black leather belt was a long metal chain. And at the end of the long metal chain was a great big bunch of keys... I was working in a prison.

This had never been a burning ambition and I'd ended up in jail, making do, because it was an easy option at the time...

My actual ambition was to be a make-up artist, but as I completed that qualification it became clear that because of my disability, a job with lots of standing wasn't feasible.

I moved into the more sedentary profession of textiles and fashion design, and I worked as a college lecturer for a long time. That was until I became a mum, and then the tug at my heartstrings at the thought of leaving my beautiful baby boy every day was just too much to bear.

I never went back after maternity leave. Instead, I entered the world of party plan make-up sales. I LOVED it! I was getting paid for playing with make-up and around for every school run. I went to all the sports days, and I was there to see my son's stage debut in his first nativity. It was perfect. I did really well and won all kinds of awards.

I even met Sir Richard Branson several times.

However, despite this outward success, the dressing nice, doing my hair and make-up every day, I was miserable on the inside.

I'd met the black dog again. I was suffering from depression, and I didn't really feel like me anymore.

I'd gained five stone during pregnancy and just hadn't been able to shift it. Firmly in the plus size category, I hated my body and never felt nice in my clothes. I wore a lot of slimming black.

The little voices in my head never had anything good to say. Why are you even bothering? You don't look nice anymore... I was in a very negative relationship with myself. I didn't feel like I was worth it.

By this time, my relationship with my husband was very negative too; I was making do. We were living separate lives.

To top this, the party plan company I'd loved working for changed direction and I wasn't even enjoying that anymore.

I was in a rut, making do, and didn't feel like myself anymore. I'd lost my identity. The creative, vibrant, sassy, confident Lisa had blended into a magnolia world, and I was bored with my lot.

Something had to change, and this is where the prison comes in. They were looking for an art teacher.

I got back in the classroom and loved it. Before long I was promoted and earning more than I'd ever earned before, with eight weeks' paid holiday a year and a fabulous pension scheme. I had my self-worth, my confidence and my sense of identity back. I felt like me again.

Pretty soon I was promoted again, but very quickly realised there would be ZERO job satisfaction.

That role, as prison education manager, began sucking the life out of me. I felt trapped, in an office, with bars on the windows, day in, day out, filling in spreadsheets.

My only chance of creativity was doodling in my notepad during the endless meetings. I was so fed up, but this time I felt trapped by the golden handcuffs of the great salary, the eight weeks' holiday a year and the fabulous pension scheme – I couldn't afford to leave.

I was incredibly unhappy. I dreaded going to work, I had a sick feeling in my stomach every night, and my self-worth and confidence took a massive dip again. This job was just not me. There was nothing about it that allowed me to be myself.

I couldn't even wear what I wanted because of the dress code and that stupid black leather belt.

Then two things happened that turned my world upside down... I had a horrible, traumatic experience at work, which led to me having a total mental breakdown, and not long after this my husband, after 23 years, admitted he didn't want to be with me anymore. He left.

Just before these two things happened, I met a woman who I think was my earth angel. We connected and quickly become good friends. She was my confidant and crutch during this really dark time of my life.

I was off work, an emotional wreck, struggling to see things in perspective. I spent a lot of time on her settee with tears, tissues and cups of tea as she used her coaching skills to guide me through making sense of everything.

One afternoon she asked. 'What would you do if you could do absolutely anything? What would make your heart sing?' and right there the concept of my business was born.

Despite the circumstances, this became a way for me to reclaim my identity. The work stuff and husband stuff left me pretty much at rock bottom but with the help of my little pal Prozac and the amazing support of friends I took back control.

Everything happens for a reason; it just might not be clear at the time.

To improve my self-worth and boost my confidence I knew I HAD to invest in myself and believe that I was worth it. No more making do.

No longer restricted by that black leather belt, I returned to dressing more creatively, loving colour and leopard print and sparkly, glittery things. I could properly be me. I decorated my bedroom with statement magenta pink flamingo wallpaper. It was about reclaiming my identity and space.

I began online dating for a bit of fun. Behind the keyboard, I was confident, fun-loving, sassy Flamingo Jo! It felt great being me again and before long I met my soul mate. We got married in May 2019, five years to the day since we had our first chat.

When I felt like I needed to rise like a phoenix from the ashes it was flamingos instead that became symbolic with my change and transformation.

All the things that I used to express my identity had gradually disappeared over the years. I'd been hiding away in the "slimming black", my wardrobe had gotten dreary, my home had become bland. My vibrant personality and joy of colour was hiding somewhere in the back of the wardrobe, just waiting to be unleashed.

All that time that I'd wasted being unhappy with my size, feeling stuck in a rut... It was as if, once I'd decided I was worth it, I began to get my mojo back.

I recognised that I could use the power of my story, plus all my knowledge and experience with colour, clothes, make-up and teaching, and bring it together into a rewarding, fulfilling business that makes a difference to the lives of other women who are also making do in some way. I traded as My Ruby Slippers Style Academy for the first five years of being in business. The name was inspired by a quote from the Wizard of Oz. 'You always had the power, my dear; you just had to learn it for yourself,' says Glinda the Good Witch to Dorothy before she returns home, enlightened, to Kansas.

I'd been fascinated by colour analysis for such a long time. My mum first had her colours done way back in the 1980s and I'd always absolutely loved it and dabbled with the theory but had never been able to afford to formally train to do it.

So, when I got an unexpected windfall, I invested that money and I trained properly in colour analysis and learned about styling. It blended perfectly with my experience of textiles and fashion and my make-up background.

I pulled it all together into my business, which is about empowering women. I teach them how to dress with confidence and enjoy self-expression through colour and clothes; to reclaim their identity. It's about compassion more than fashion. When you stand in front of your wardrobe, frustrated because you have nothing to wear, often it's not just about the clothes.

So many women feel like they're in a rut, especially when they get to 40 or 50 years old. The kids are getting older but they're possibly looking after elderly parents now; their body shape has changed, and menopause is knocking, and they're sometimes experiencing divorce, redundancy or workplace trauma, like I did.

These life experiences conspire to knock your confidence, but by harnessing the power of colour and clothes you can alter so much about who you are, how you feel and how you show up in the world.

You can absolutely be who you want to be and express yourself, whatever your age, shape or size.

You might not realise that you can improve your boundaries – I didn't.

Looking back over my life, I can now see how I've allowed circumstances and events to impact on my feelings of self-worth. Like the disfiguring scars from all the surgery I've had on my hip, which look like a shark bit a chunk out of the left-hand side of my body. Or the limp I've had most of my life. Or the fact that I've been conscious of my weight since the age of nine and spent a long time worrying about being fat (even when I wasn't). And then the two car accidents – the catalyst for my clinical depression in later years.

Because of this, amongst other things, I've had boyfriends who didn't deserve me, put up with bosses and colleagues who treated me badly and worn clothes just because they fit me.

I spent a lot of time being the statue more often than the pigeon instead of the flamingo I was born to be.

Statues are not colourful, and they are stuck in one place and get shit on. Pigeons are grey with a bit of colour around their neck but nothing too adventurous; they blend into the crowd. Whereas the flamingo is bold, colourful and proud, and stands out from the crowd.

I allowed myself to make do and put up with stuff. Not anymore!

Now it's my passion to help other women reclaim their identity and boost their self-worth and confidence; no more making do.

It's my absolute mission to help women shift from feeling drab to fab, okay to awesome and help them become the flamingo amongst the flock of pigeons.

So now you know a bit more of my back story and why I do what I do. Turn the page and let's get cracking!

Don't
MAKE
DO

Project FAB Framework

Let's Get to the Nitty Gritty

This book is all about my Project FAB! framework and it will provide you with tips and advice so you can create your own pathway by putting theory into action.

There are four elements to the framework and these elements run through all my work, whether it's my blog on my website, my social media posts, my self-study courses, or my group and 121 sessions. These concepts have been tweaked and refined but the core aims have remained constant and how much detail/depth we go into very much depends on the individual.

These are:

1. **STYLE** - This element is about working out why you like what you like and what your personal style actually is.

2. **SHADES** - This element is about working out your best colours to wear and how to put them together so they truly enhance your features.

3. **SHAPE** - This element is where you learn about your body type, shape and proportions so you can select styles that work with you rather than against your natural shape.

4. **SUSTAIN** - This element is where you begin to analyse HOW to make your wardrobe work for you in a practical way so the contents are earning their keep.

Project FAB! Framework – Putting YOU at the Centre

Let me expand. Project FAB! is about putting you at the centre of your own project with a view to projecting your best, most fabulous self. Think back to your school days and being set a homework project for the summer holidays. You probably had to do some research, planning and reflecting.

This book has been created to get you started on the most important project you will ever work on – yourself. I'm no psychologist, but I know for sure that your personal appearance can impact on how you feel. To be successful, my framework relies on you taking action in the following areas:

- **Being more you** – this is about exploring your identity and being more yourself than you've ever been before

- **Believing you're worth it** – this is about being willing to set boundaries and putting yourself at the front of the queue

- **Believing you can do it** – this is about having the self-belief and confidence to make the transformation you desire

You get to choose what FAB means to you:

F – fabulous, flamboyant, funky, fascinating, fierce, fresh, fashionable, fun

A – adventurous, awesome, authentic, amazing, aligned, ace, ageless, aglow

B – bold, bright, brilliant, beautiful, ballsy, balanced, best, blooming

You can pick from my list or make up your own version.

TASK: What's Your FAB?

Foundation level task: Choose three words to make your version of FAB.

Advanced level task: Choose three words to make your version of FAB and write a short sentence to describe what each word means to you.

Best practice level task: Choose three words to make your version of FAB and write a short sentence to describe what each word means to you. Then journal about the outcome you'd like when you've worked through this Project FAB! book. Think about how you'll know that you achieved your desired outcome. What will have changed that tells you that your investment in this project worked?

What's your FAB?

F

A

B

Style

First Impressions

'Style is much more interesting than fashion.'

Marc Jacobs

The first element in Project FAB! is about working out why you like what you like and what YOUR personal style is.

When you have this bit sussed, suddenly it becomes clear why you have things in your wardrobe that you never wear and why that necklace that Aunty Bridget bought you for your 40th birthday has never seen the light of day. You'll be able to stop wrestling with those hangers in your wardrobe as you no longer compromise and have a streamlined wardrobe that makes you smile when you open it.

Style Speaks

'How you present yourself is how people will value you.'

Paul Arden

In this section we are looking at first impressions and why they are important. It used to be said that we had seven seconds to make a first impression, but the latest research I could find was in *Psychological Science Magazine*, July 2006 and it had reduced to one tenth of a second! That was years ago, so I think it's fair to expect that by now we've got even less time to make a good impression.

Think about all the different places, especially in business, where you make a first impression. It could be on social media, it could be your website, it might your profile pictures on LinkedIn or Facebook or any of the places where you are showing up daily online as well as in real life. When you turn up at events, either social occasions or for work, people make judgments and even though none of us like to think we're being "judgy", we are. We are *all* judging *all* the time, whether it's a conscious thing or not.

When we see someone for the first time, we make decisions about how well educated they are, their social status, etc. We create a subconscious opinion about them during that first encounter and our first impression is formed. We might also make conscious opinions too. The important thing with this first impression stuff is to acknowledge that it really does matter because first impressions last.

There is scientific proof that we very seldom change what we think about somebody once we have formed that first impression. Instead, our reticular filter kicks in and we start looking for evidence to support our opinion. It's a bit like when you're buying a red car and then suddenly you notice how many red cars there are on the road.

TASK: First Impressions

Foundation level task: For each pair of glasses below, choose three words to describe the type of person who'd wear them Think about what they might be like as a person in terms of their personality, e.g. outgoing, extrovert, introvert; maybe you could even think about the kind of job they do. Don't think too hard about it – go with your first impression.

Advanced level task: Choose three words to describe the type of person who'd wear each pair of glasses and write a short sentence to explain why you chose those words.

Best practice level task: Choose three words to describe the type of person who'd wear the glasses and write a short sentence to explain why you chose those words. Then journal around how you feel about being judged and how "judgy" you are as a person.

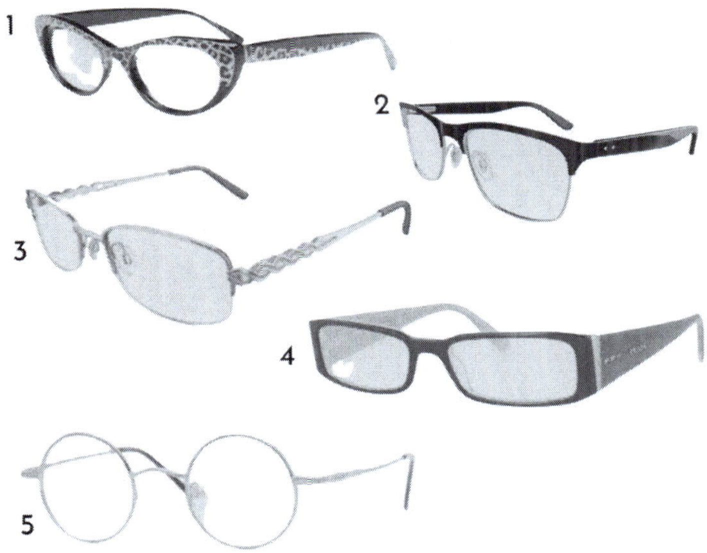

My first impressions are:

1

2

3

4

5

I've done this exercise with hundreds of people in various workshops and presentations. The words they use are always very much in the same vein. It's proof that your style says something about you before you ever speak.

The words that are usually fed back are generally:

1. female, extrovert, creative; sexy often gets added into the mix too
2. male, confident, serious, business-like
3. female, feminine, quiet, thoughtful
4. female, confident, assertive, no nonsense
5. male or female, shy, artistic, introvert

How do they match up with your perceptions and the words you have written down?

I like to have a bit of variety with my specs and change things up a bit, so I always buy two pairs at a time. Two of the pairs in the exercise – #1 and #4 – were mine in around 2010. With my job as prison education manager, I needed gravitas and to be taken seriously by the prisoners, prison officers and my teaching staff as well as the senior management team of the prison. I attended meetings with the prison governors, who were often male, pale and stale. Had I rocked up in my leopard print glasses, which were quirky and a bit more fun, they may have perceived me quite differently to how I turned up in my quite serious, more business-like glasses. I felt the leopard print ones were a little bit too outrageous and gave off more of a funky vibe, so I didn't wear them for work.

Takeaways

- First impressions last
- We all judge – even if we think we don't

Visual Communication

'Style is a way to say who you are without having to speak.'

Rachel Zoe

This quote sums up perfectly what style is as far as I'm concerned when we're looking at the language of colour and clothes.

Here are a couple more pictures.

These photos were taken on the same day by the same photographer within an hour or so of each other, but they give off very different vibes. Thinking back to the first impression stuff, the different vibe I'm giving off in each photograph is down to the fact that I've changed my clothes; the backgrounds have also changed slightly. Then it's about the look on my face, the way I'm standing, my posture. They convey very different messages.

I posted these on LinkedIn and Facebook and asked people for their response to each picture. There were lots of comments about me looking like a rock star or a pop star, unapproachable and not particularly friendly in the first photo, while the majority of people felt I appeared friendlier and more approachable in the second picture. It's said a picture paints a thousand words. I want you to really think about what your profile pictures are saying about you – it is definitely food for thought.

Working in a prison environment was quite different to anything I'd ever done before. I felt quite restricted by the dress code, by what I could wear and what I couldn't. There were lots of things I needed to consider when I was getting dressed.

One of the things was that I had to wear a black leather belt with a leather bum bag attached to it, which is where my keys went. This meant that my tops had to be short enough for me to quickly get access to my belt, but I also wanted to cover my belly, so my tops had to be a very specific length. I also didn't want anything too low cut, or anything you could see down or through.

I couldn't even wear my scarves! If you follow me on social media, you'll know most days I'm wearing a scarf. But in the prison, I couldn't wear them because they could be used as a weapon against me. I could have been strangled or tied up using my own scarf if I was taken hostage. (Necklaces were fine because they would tend to break.)

I didn't want anything that drew attention to my curves (AKA my enormous mahoosive boobs!) either. So, with all these restrictions on how I could dress, it was very difficult for me to really say who I was as a person. I had very dark purple dye on my hair, but it only really looked a little bit purple in certain lights; it wasn't anywhere near as purple as I've had it since.

Along with the depression I've already mentioned, this job very much left me feeling that I wasn't really me and I lost my identity a little bit again. Style is about expressing who you are – inside and out.

TASK: Visual Communication

Foundation level task: Think about your profile picture on social media or a recent photograph. Choose three words that you think it conveys.

Advanced level task: Think about your profile picture on social media. Choose three words that you think it conveys. What are the specific things about your profile picture that have made you think of these words?

Best practice level task: Think about your profile picture on social media. Choose three words that you think it conveys. What are the specific things about your profile picture that have made you think of these words? Look at the profile pictures of other people you are connected to. Journal around what you like and dislike in profile pictures. What are the recurring themes? Are you inspired to make changes based on this exercise?

Stick your photo here

What 3 words are you conveying?

1

2

3

Takeaways

- A picture paints a thousand words
- The devil is in the detail

Style Personality

'To me, style is all about expressing your individuality freely and courageously.'

Timothy John

Do you feel too old to follow fashion but still want to look on trend? Do you sometimes worry about looking like mutton dressed as lamb... or go the other way and worry about turning into your mother? You might see stuff you like in magazines, but don't know if you're too old to go in "those" shops, or how to incorporate trendy stuff into your outfits without looking and feeling a bit daft.

Mostly when I work with clients who feel this way it's because they don't know what their *style personality* type is. They can describe the type of clothes they like best, but whenever they've decided to try something different it's ended up in the back of the wardrobe with the tags still on; they've got it out and tried it on loads of times but never actually got around to wearing it. Or they wore it once for a night out, but it didn't quite feel right so they never wore it again.

You will have had some clothes in your wardrobe that you've worn until they fell apart and others like new that you've put in the charity bag. When this happens it's usually because you've veered away from your innate style personality archetype.

This element of my Project FAB! framework is about the importance of understanding your innate style personality and how it can save you time, money and even stop you from feeling guilty!! Read on to appreciate why, even though you love that Joe Browns tunic on your sister, it just doesn't look or feel right on you.

Fashion Says: 'Me Too!' and Style Says: 'Only Me.'

Understanding your style personality is ESSENTIAL to having a stylish wardrobe that is just right for you... It's the thing that will prevent you from buying things you never wear and help you make more informed choices when you are shopping – hence it's also money-saving.

It also helps you save time because you understand why you'll never find anything in that particular shop so it's not worth even going in for a browse; you'll never waste time thinking about what you "should" be wearing for that party or wedding because once you have your style personality sussed it all makes sense.

Once I got into this style personality thing, I realised that it is a key to unlocking a lot of stuff around the clothes that are languishing at the back of the wardrobe. There are a lot of 'Aha!' moments when I talk about it with my clients. Quite often we can like things that are outside of our innate style personality – things other people are wearing, or that we see in shops or magazines or on the telly. But just because you like something doesn't mean it's going to be right for you.

Style Personality Archetypes

I work with six style personality archetypes. Most of us will have one dominant type with a secondary one, and this determines our personal style. It takes into consideration things like whether you prefer minimalist or more flamboyant clothes, pretty and feminine, tailored and simple, flowing and tactile fabrics, pattern and colours etc. Even your hair and attitude to make-up are considered. There'll be certain brands and shops that you are drawn to because your style personality type matches their target market profile.

Sometimes elements of a different style personality type will come to the fore depending on what we're doing, or the occasion. We might bring in the others occasionally, but we'll have one main innate style personality that dictates why we like what we like. When you understand what the qualities are in garments and styles that work for your style personality type, it helps you make fewer mistakes.

Just like people who have very different behavioural personality types and might not get on, it can be the same with style personalities. When you choose items that cross over style personality types it can create disharmony with your overall look and things will not look or feel quite right. For example, you like something, you buy it, you put it in your wardrobe but when you get it out to wear something about it doesn't feel right – you can't quite put your finger on what it is, but you know it's not right. So, you take it off and you hang it back up in the wardrobe and there it stays. As an example of what I mean, imagine a bohemian, fringed, soft suede handbag; it wouldn't look quite right with a simple, classic shift dress and smart court shoes. This is because they belong in two different categories of style personality.

The trick is to analyse your personal style to find out WHY you like something. There will be recurring themes within your wardrobe, things that repeat in a variety of items of clothing. If you were to ask yourself what it is you like about something, what words crop up? Write them down and you'll start to understand what you prefer and why.

Style Personality Quiz

I have a quiz to help you understand your style personality type. It is one of those mostly A, mostly B type quizzes. Very occasionally someone comes out with a jumble of all the letters and no clearly defined style. This means either they are very confused and can have extreme wardrobe wobbles, never really knowing what to wear OR they are extremely confident in their clothes choices and have their very own unique style (and don't need me!).

Choose ONE option per question.

1. How do you like to wear colour?

   a. Coordinated with quiet, understated neutrals
   b. Sophisticated shades mixed with light neutrals
   c. High contrast and bold patterns are good
   d. Simple, muted colour combinations inspired by nature
   e. Gentle, pretty, soft, pastels and tints
   f. Interesting, imaginative, experimental combinations

2. What kind of shopper are you?

   a. I am an investment buyer of timeless pieces
   b. I think about what I already have in my wardrobe
   c. I buy something unusual with a splash of colour
   d. I'm quickly in and out, buying basics for all seasons
   e. I love small boutiques and a personal service
   f. I head to the flea market for funky, unique finds

3. Which of these do you identify with most closely?

   a. Timeless, simple, tailored, elegant, classic, sophisticated
   b. Contemporary, current, coordinated, tonal, polished, chic
   c. Bold, strong, striking, confident, attention-grabbing, edgy
   d. Understated, simple, easy, functional, relaxed, casual
   e. Gentle, soft, sensitive, pretty, cute, feminine

f. Creative, unconventional, whimsical, spirited, unique, unusual

4. How does pattern feature in your wardrobe?

a. Not much of it – fine stripes or small polka dots
b. Geometrics and stylised designs in sophisticated colours
c. Large scale, bold, high contrast, animal print
d. Stripes and checks
e. Texture, florals, butterflies, lace
f. Abstract, whimsical, ethnic, digital print

5. What features most in your wardrobe?

a. Simple styles in good quality fabrics that never date
b. Classy prints and sophisticated colours in soft, quality fabrics
c. Eye-catching, bold colours and fabrics
d. Jeans and practical, comfortable tops in natural fabrics
e. Embellished tops and dresses in soft, tactile fabrics
f. A cornucopia of whimsical styles with a boho vibe

6. What is your special occasion outfit?

a. A classic little black dress
b. Elegant styling with accessories, hair and make-up
c. Something striking – definitely has the wow factor

d. Aaaaaggghhhhh, I hate dressing up
e. Luxurious fabrics with details – ruffles, bows, frills
f. A unique look that has taken time to put together

7. What are the most important elements of fit for you?
   a. Structured but not tight, nothing sloppy
   b. Fitted and softly structured
   c. Form fitting to show off assets
   d. Looser fit, comfort is key
   e. Cut to show a feminine shape
   f. That the overall look fits my vision

8. What kind of jewellery do you like?
   a. Simple and fine, precious metal, rarely change it
   b. Good quality, clean lines, finishes the look
   c. Bold and chunky conversation starters
   d. If I wear it – shell, leather, semi-precious stones
   e. Intricate, detailed and coordinates with outfit
   f. Unusual – I collect it

9. What is your attitude towards make-up?
   a. I keep to the same simple routine
   b. I love it and keep up to date

c. I have my own definite look
d. The bare minimum or none
e. I wouldn't leave the house without it
f. I like to experiment

10. What type of hairstyle do you have?
    a. Neat, well maintained and healthy looking
    b. Stylish, contemporary, well groomed
    c. Colourful, edgy, highly styled
    d. Low maintenance, natural looking
    e. Long, loose, soft and feminine
    f. I experiment with it

Tot up your answers by counting the number of As, Bs, Cs etc., and then read the results. Can you recognise your primary and secondary archetype?

Remember – we all have a primary type, usually complemented by a secondary one (occasionally a third). This is just a fun quiz that will give you an idea of your style personality mix. It's one of the keys to ending wardrobe mistakes and can be very illuminating. When you stray too far from your innate style personality, that's when the clothes languish in the wardrobe.

Mostly As: Classic

You are ladylike, elegant and truly appreciate that less is more. You prefer quality over quantity and believe in spending a little extra to get beautifully cut, well-fitting garments. You like good tailoring and prefer simple, clean lines. You don't really do printed or patterned fabrics except the occasional stripe, small polka dot or discreet motif. You aren't into anything flashy or brash. You aren't comfortable with fussy details such as frills and ruffles and feel conspicuous in anything bold or brightly coloured. Your worst nightmare is to be seen in anything that looks cheap or scruffy. Beware of looking old before your time and blending into the background.

Mostly Bs: Elegant Chic

You are self-assured, confident and independent, admired for your sleek, chic, well turned-out sense of style. You like to stand out in the crowd for your attention to detail without being flashy. Simple, clean-cut shapes and styles with a bit of a twist are your preferred choice. You aren't afraid of colour but stick to complementary tones within your carefully put-together outfit. You love to build an outfit around a hero or statement piece of clothing; you're not afraid of pattern or unusual details. You could never be called a slave to fashion as your individuality shines through in your unique styling. Your worst nightmare would be having to wear neon synthetic fabric. Beware of seeming aloof.

Mostly Cs: Dramatic

You love to seek out unusual pieces, preferring to create your own style whilst keeping an eye on trends and being current. You love to mix up your outfits by searching out exclusive, distinctive pieces. You are forward thinking and adventurous. Sometimes you are uncomfortable in your clothes and shoes, but it is a small price to pay for looking amazing. You would rather be over the top and overdressed than blend in with the crowd. Your worst nightmare would be turning up to an event and someone else being in the same outfit. Beware of looking like you have tried too hard to be "different".

Mostly D:s Relaxed/Natural

You love to be comfortable and feel relaxed in your clothes. You like simple, no-fuss styles in natural fabrics such as cotton and linen. You enjoy quality low key separates and aren't overly concerned with fiddly details. You are great at layering in a loose, unstructured way and value comfort and functionality in your wardrobe. You enjoy teaming soft, muted prints and patterns, stripes or checks in a casual manner with jeans or combat trousers, accessorising with leather, natural stones or shell jewellery that is subtly stylish. Your worst nightmare is formal dressing for a wedding or black-tie event. Beware not being taken seriously in a formal business context and experiment with finding a way to adapt your natural, relaxed style for formal occasions.

Mostly Es: Romantic/Feminine

You are sexy and womanly, empathetic and sensitive. Your clothes often have a story attached to them. You love soft, floaty feminine styles, often in pastel colours, with delicate detailing such as ruffles, frills, pleats or lace. Texture and tactile fabrics are where you are naturally drawn: silk, chiffon, velvet, tweed, corduroy etc. You prefer drapey fabrics with a softly fitted silhouette, asymmetric hemlines and full sleeves. Your worst nightmare would be having to wear a dark, formal, structured business suit. Beware of not being taken seriously in business because you look "girly".

Mostly Fs: Eclectic/Creative

You are unconventional, expressive and experimental with your style. You dress according to your mood of the day, inspired by something you see in a magazine or by a song on the radio. You may have a timeless look and err towards a quirky, bohemian style of dressing. You treat getting dressed like building up the layers in a painting and take it seriously. You like to seek out unusual items and combine them in unexpected ways, adding things you love to your eclectic collection as you find them in vintage shops, budget brands as well as the high street. Your worst nightmare is having to conform; having to wear a uniform would just be the pits. Beware of putting too many statements in one outfit and looking like you've been in the dressing-up box.

TASK: Style Personality Quiz

Foundation level task: Take the quiz.

Advanced level task: Take the quiz. Reflect on why you chose your answers.

Best practice level task: Take the quiz. Reflect on why you chose your answers. Journal around your answers and how the description of the archetypes make you feel. Do you feel like you'd want to make changes to your style based on those descriptions?

Tot up your scores

A B C D E F

My primary archetype is:

My secondary archetype is:

Takeaways

- Your style speaks
- More than three archetypes = confused or confident

Style Personality Disharmony

Your style personality is relevant to every aspect of your appearance. It even works with accessories – jewellery, bags, shoes etc.

Many years ago, before I knew about the style personalities, I was given an expensive gift, a teensy, weensy diamond pendant set on a delicate gold chain with matching earrings. It was very pretty, and it cost over £100, but it was simply not "me".

As you know, I'm a big girl and this teeny tiny little diamond necklace just disappeared on my frame. I'm also quite a dramatic dresser and there was no drama around this little gold jewellery set. The fact that it was expensive made me feel bad not wearing it, but I also had a toddler and if he pulled that little chain, it would snap... There was a lot of guilt attached to this gift for a very long time.

I never wore the pendant and it ended up in a bedroom drawer, never seeing the light of day. I felt guilty about not wearing it until I realised that it was incongruous with my style personality. I'm a Dramatic and this delicate set was more suited to a Classic. The gifter had chosen something that suited her style personality, not mine.

Fast forward a few years to when I was working in the prison. Because the dress code meant I couldn't add colour and interest to my outfits, I wore coordinating earrings and necklaces every day as my way of expressing my personality and identity. I had lots of matching earring and necklace sets to suit my dramatic style personality. One Mother's Day my son bought me a necklace and earrings set, costume jewellery; it was purple, and I like purple. But it was flowery and had loads of ornate decoration that was quite feminine and twee; just not my style at all. I've still got it – I can't throw it away, because it was given with love. But it's just not something that I feel comfortable wearing. It's very pretty, but just a bit too girly and "romantic" for me.

TASK: Disharmony

Foundation level task: Now you've done the quiz and have some insight into your style personality, list three examples of outfits/items you knew weren't quite right and now recognise it's because of style personality disharmony.

Advanced level task: Now you've done the quiz and have some insight into your style personality, list three examples of outfits/items you knew weren't quite right and now recognise it's because of style personality disharmony. Reflect on why the items were disharmonious.

Best practice level task: Now you've done the quiz and have some insight into your style personality, list three examples of outfits/items you knew weren't quite right and now recognise it's because of style personality disharmony. Reflect on why you consider the items to be disharmonious. Journal around your answers and think about how that disharmony makes you feel when it's happening.

My disharmonious items/outfits:

1

2

3

Takeaways

- Disharmony can be why things don't feel right
- Don't feel guilty if gifts aren't your style

Style Personality Summary

Once you understand your style personality type it's easier to develop and create your own signature style and improve your image confidence. Becoming aware of your authentic personal style means you can get dressed in confidence on a daily basis. It doesn't mean that things are boring, or you must get stuck in a rut and only wear certain styles; it is about recognising the qualities of the things you like. No more wardrobe wobbles because you have your own guidelines to follow. You save time because you "own" your look and getting dressed becomes easier.

It also saves you loads of time when you are shopping because you aren't wandering around looking at things that don't suit you and will end up at the back of the wardrobe. You save money because you wear everything that you buy.

The best thing about honouring your personal style rather than fashion is that you don't need to worry about what is in fashion. You can nod to trends but know that you will stick to items that are a good fit for your personality. For example, if suede is a key trend this season you could choose a suede item that fits your personality. It might be classic court shoes, a biker jacket or a fringed handbag.

Your personal style will continue evolving with time. It doesn't have to become stagnant, but you will benefit from making informed decisions when you buy new clothes.

TIP: If you are experimenting and trying something new it can sometimes feel like quite a stretch even if it is spot-on for you. Because it is different, your brain can battle with the change and that can feel like quite a stretch outside of your current comfort zone. This is when I recommend "the supermarket test". This is when you wear the new item out for a brief trip to the supermarket. It's a good place to be out and about in public but you're not going to be there ages if you start to feel self-conscious. Then you increase the time of wearing it incrementally until it feels natural.

Style Recipe

'Style is something each of us already has; all we need to do is find it.'

Diane von Furstenberg

Putting an outfit together isn't just about getting dressed and covering your body. It's about saying who you are through how you look – and, surprise, surprise, you are totally in control of that.

The good news is that you can hone the language of colour and clothes, so you are saying something about who you are before you even open your mouth.

Most of us learn to dress ourselves before we start school. But that doesn't always mean that you know how to put an outfit together that expresses your identity and is authentically aligned with you as an individual.

Imagine getting dressed each day in an outfit that:

- really suits you and makes you look good and feel fab
- conveys your identity and expresses who you are as a person
- makes you feel empowered and confident
- suits whatever you have got happening that day

You might be so stuck in a rut with what you are used to wearing that you've lost your confidence to try anything new or different that varies too much from your norm. This section is definitely not about putting you in a box or restricting you to a self-imposed uniform every day. Nailing this will ultimately give you a sense of freedom and excitement as you are owning and rocking your look on a daily basis, whatever the situation or environment. Your style recipe is all about providing that next level of *comfydence*.

Comfydence

Comfydence is one of my made-up words – it's a cross between comfortable and confident. It's something to aspire to when you are putting an outfit together. It's the aftermath of a *stylegasm* – another of my made-up words. You have a stylegasm when your outfit makes you want to twirl around and keep looking at yourself in the mirror. You can't stop smiling and might even squeal with excitement. It's when you look and feel a million dollars and it ticks ALL the boxes of your style recipe.

Your style recipe is about your essence; it's very personal to you and encapsulates your identity, how you see yourself and how you want to be perceived. You then translate it into your personal appearance, and it gets tweaked depending on the flavour required for each day.

It's just like cooking. You have your basic recipe; you know the ingredients needed and you can experiment with the finer details, adding spices and putting different twists on it depending on your mood. You'll be able to put together a cohesive wardrobe that reflects your personality and lifestyle and can be dialled up and down to suit the occasion.

So, how do you go about creating your style recipe?

Assess your personal style as it stands currently. Think about how you appear today, and what your clothes say about you now, and then consider what you want them to say about you in the future.

Point A is your starting style. Point B is where you are aspiring to be. How much of a gap is there between the two? The gap between the two will vary from person to person and with the four step Project FAB! framework you can work out what needs to happen to bridge the gap.

If the gap is enormous or seems a stretch too far then remember, this is a journey. Whilst B maybe your final destination you can also create some pitstops or milestones to celebrate along the way. For example, you might want to get your whole wardrobe sorted for every occasion and the first milestone could be to get your work wardrobe sorted, then casual, then smart. You get the idea.

Remember to be realistic and authentic. Your style recipe is not just about your public persona. The aim is for it to be sustainable across all areas of your life.

Your style recipe reflects how you want to be perceived. What action do you need to take so that you and other people see you that way? It's not about you having a makeover and looking like someone else. It's about being more you than you've ever been before. No more making do or pretending to be someone you are not.

WARNING! I know someone who had beautiful naturally wavy hair and usually wore just a little bit of make-up. She had a photo shoot for her business and was primped and preened by a hair and make-up artist; she had the full works with perfect foundation, contouring etc., straightened her hair into a sleek bob – she looked amazing! However, it wasn't how she normally looked, nor could she recreate it daily on her own. Her photos came out brilliantly, but she didn't look like herself at all. The images were so incongruent with everything she usually represented in terms of her business that she didn't seem authentic. Nor did people recognise her initially once they met in real life after seeing the photo first.

This kind of thing can, at its worst, make some people think you are fake or putting on an act. Either way, it does not bode well for building connection and trust – least of all with yourself, when you look at the photo and other people tell you how lovely you look but you don't even recognise yourself. None of that is great for the relationship you have with yourself.

Style Recipe Inspiration

Having a background in art, I know that I gain inspiration from nature and the things around me. I might see a flower and the colour or pattern might inspire me to create an outfit that reflects the essence of that.

This concept might be new to you, so be kind and have fun noticing what you are drawn to.

You could start with your own wardrobe. Think about the qualities and properties of your favourite items of clothing or accessories. Notice if you prefer plain conservative neutrals or bold clashing colours, soft and tactile or firmer, more structured fabric. Make a list of everything that you know you love and brings you joy. If you are struggling, then refer to the questions in the style personality quiz if you need help getting started.

Think about things you find pleasing to look at. It could be things around your home or garden, pieces of artwork, images from magazines. Jot down words that describe why you like these things. What are the properties that attract you? I remember one client had never really thought about what or who inspired her. Once we got talking, she discovered she had a favourite chair, and she loved the colours and the swirls. The colours became the inspiration for her first capsule wardrobe, which I will tell you more about later.

You could include brands you like and what you admire about them. Do you notice recurring themes? It might be bold colours, simple clean lines, texture, pattern etc. You could use a Pinterest board or create a collage if you're a visual person – either a digital one or "old school" with cutting and sticking. Flicking through magazines and noticing what you are drawn to without overthinking it can be a quick way to notice what you are naturally drawn to.

Think about your personality traits and jot down some words that describe you as a person. If you find this hard then perhaps consider who you would like to be or how you would like others to see you.

It can take a bit of time and effort to do this process in depth, but it is worth it because your style recipe becomes more about having a check-in process with how you're looking. It will span the different aspects of your life.

TASK: Style Recipe

Foundation level task: Jot down 3-5 words to use for your style recipe. Consider how you might express these words with your appearance.

Advanced level task: Jot down 3-5 words to use for your style recipe and a sentence about what each one means to you. Consider how you might express these words with your appearance.

Best practice level task: Create a list of words that reflect how you want to be perceived by others – check out synonyms in the thesaurus – and make a note about what each of your words means to you. Whittle down your list to 3-5 words to become your style recipe. Consider how you might express these words with your appearance.

My Style Recipe words are:

1

2

3

4

5

Having identified your innate style personality, it makes sense for your style recipe to be congruent with that.

For example, it might be that one of your words might be "creative" but when you look at the styles and shapes of the clothes and the colours you wear, they might be quite conservative and classic, therefore people are not going to perceive you as being a creative person.

You may want to come across as warm and approachable ... or proficient and serious might be more your vibe. Just as no one is going to think of you as creative and quirky if you rock up in a grey business suit, neither are you going to seem warm and approachable if you're wearing a very high contrast outfit like a black jacket and white top, as this would stand for authority and power. Think police uniforms, prison officers, judges etc.

It could just be that changing your jacket to a bolder colour or adding quirky buttons would make you look more creative. A crafty designer friend of mine added small pink poms poms around the edges and hem of a classic style jacket and completely changed the feel of it.

This is now your time to experiment and play around to see what works for you to give you more stylegasms and comfydence.

My Style Recipe

My style recipe is vibrant, fun, stylish, creative and sassy. I have a vision of what these words mean to me so when I'm getting dressed, that's how I want to be perceived.

- Vibrant = lively, colourful, energetic
- Fun = light-hearted, I don't take myself too seriously
- Stylish = I walk the walk and talk the talk, I have my own look
- Creative = I like to inspire others to break the mould

- Sassy = confident, a bit bold, cheeky at times

For me, this recipe runs across everything in my brand; it's not just about how I look. It's about my posts on social media, it's about the tone of voice of everything that I write and so on. This way people get a feel for me and know whether there's a connection, whether they resonate with me, whether they think I'm a good fit for them, etc. There are lots of other people doing the kind of stuff that I do, but nobody else will do it my way because they're not me. It's all about my vibe attracting my tribe.

When I Forgot About My Style Recipe

When my sister was getting married in 2015, I panicked and temporarily forgot about my style recipe. I started looking at the special occasion section in John Lewis and the JD Williams catalogue. As I browsed the pastel-coloured lace ensembles that were SO NOT ME, I gave my head a wobble and checked in with myself. I realised what was happening: this day was really important, and that sense of occasion had thrown me off track. I actually ended up wearing a 1950s-style dress, complete with petticoat (very me), and felt like the dog's bollocks! If that can happen to me – and I do this stuff for a living – then you can be excused if it takes you a while to get the hang of perfecting your recipe. Just keep practising.

Takeaways

- Your style recipe will give you comfydence
- It often evolves over time

Embrace

the

JOURNEY

Shades

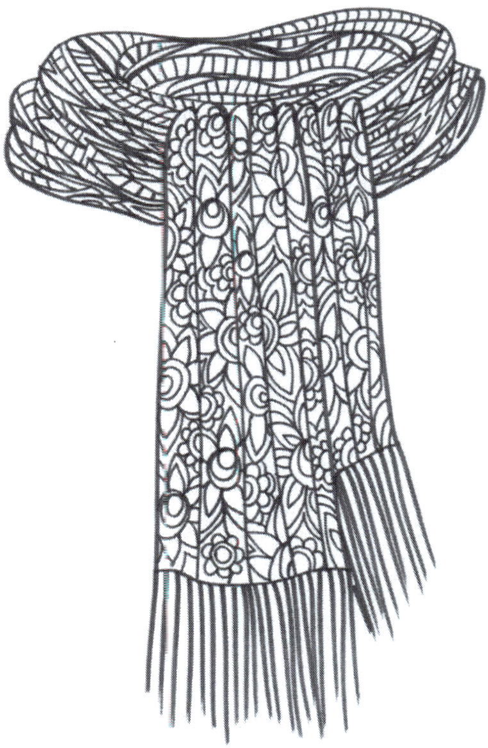

Colour Talks

'The best colour in the world is one that looks good on you.'

Coco Chanel

This element is about working out YOUR best colours to wear and how to put them together, so they truly ENHANCE your features.

When you have your colour palette sorted you will save time and money because the items in your wardrobe will all coordinate beautifully, shopping becomes easier and more focused PLUS you'll have a radiance about your skin and your eyes will sparkle. You'll be leaving the boring black behind as you feel invigorated and excited to bring colour into your world.

Whilst I cannot provide you with a personal and bespoke colour analysis, I'll share with you how to conduct a basic seasonal self-assessment. It's different from having a professional colour analysis reading with me, but you will definitely get an idea of which colours suit you best. Of course, if you do want to have my professional perspective, I offer an online assessment where you send me your photos and I conduct a full colour analysis reading.

Learning about your signature colours, i.e. the colours that suit you best, and how to rescue clothes that are not in your best colour can provide easy wins for everybody and can make a big difference to how you choose and wear colour.

So, if you've got a wardrobe full of clothes that you know are not in the right colours for you, or you feel they might be quite draining, I'll share some tips and hints about how to make them work. It's not about getting rid of everything that doesn't suit you – it's about making it work for you.

Season-Savvy Colour Analysis

Colour analysis was big in the 80s. Having your "colours done" was a thing for the ladies that lunched. I was fascinated by it even then and remember my mum getting herself done. She had a little wallet of fabric swatches that she carried around in her handbag and checked things against when she was shopping.

Colour analysis is a process based on analysing your skin tone, hair and eye colour and using that analysis to figure out which colours are going to suit you best. There are a couple of different systems, but the concept is the "right" colours will give you a glow and the wrong colours make you look tired, drained and old – and who wants that?

If you've ever googled it, chances are the two big names that crop up are House of Colour and Colour Me Beautiful. Then of course there are the independents like me, doing our own thing, who are not linked to a franchise.

Everyone can wear most colours, but the analysis systems break it down into the nuance of undertone, depth and intensity. When you wear colours that reflect your natural colouring there is a harmony about you, particularly in the portrait area i.e. your head and shoulders.

Colour analysis isn't about restricting your personal choice or making you wear colours you don't like. It is much more about finding out which colours really enhance your natural radiance and how to wear colour rather than rigidly sticking to a palette of specific tints, tones and shades.

When I talk about colours suiting you, it's all about what is near your face. It's like when you held a buttercup under your chin as a kid; it's about how the colour reflects upwards. The colour will cast flattering light or unflattering shadows depending on your skin tone.

Here are a few reasons why colour can boost your personal style and self-image confidence:

- Your skin will look clearer and more radiant when you wear your best colours, giving you a glow, and people may comment on how well you are looking.

- The colour of your eyes will seem brighter and more vibrant.

- If you wear make-up, you'll need less as your skin tone looks more even.

- Wearing your best colours (particularly near your face) really can take years off you as the colour works with your natural skin tone and eliminates shadows.

- You save time when you're shopping as you can be focused; you can scan a shop for colours in your palette and disregard the rest.

- It will save you time as your wardrobe is more coordinated and you can confidently mix and match separates as you get ready each morning.

- You save money as your wardrobe becomes more wearable – fewer items but worn more often.

- Shopping for clothes becomes easier because you really know what you are looking for and what suits you; you make confident choices.

The Different Colour Analysis Systems

There are two main colour analysis systems, the seasonal system and the tonal system. I have trained in both. The theory in either system results in a group of colours that will suit you best based on the combination of the colour of your hair, eyes and skin tones.

The seasonal colour analysis system has four main categories - spring, summer, autumn and winter. It has nothing to do with when you are born but more about the colours we (in the northern hemisphere) associate with the changing seasons. You might have heard people say they've had their colours "done" and they are a "summer" or an "autumn".

- Spring colours are fresh and bright; think about daffodils and other flowers bursting into life.

- Summer colours have a softer slightly dusky quality, like the colours of sweet peas.

- Autumn colours are reminiscent of the rich tones found in the colour of leaves as they drop.

- Winter colours are crisp and clear, stark in contrast and jewel tones.

I originally trained in the seasonal system but found the resources restrictive. So, in 2019 I retrained in a more sophisticated tonal system that gives me more nuanced results. For the purposes of your self-assessment though I am going to walk you through a simple version of the seasonal method, because it's a great starting point.

Colour Theory

Before we move onto the self-assessment, I think it's important for me to introduce you to some basic colour theory and the colour wheel. You will have probably encountered it in the first instance at infant school.

The colour wheel is basically a circular rainbow where the colours complete a circle and blend into each other. For example, red moves through to orange, to yellow to green, to blue to purple and back to red.

Every colour on the colour wheel can be made by mixing the three primary colours together. The primary colours are red, yellow and blue.

In the simplest of terms:

- warm colours = reds, yellows and oranges
- cool colours = blues, purples and greens

Note: there are warm and cool versions of every colour except orange. The reason for this is because of how you create the secondary colours. Secondary colours are what you get when you mix two primaries together. The reason why you can't have a cool orange is because:

Blue (cool) + yellow (warm) = green. If you add more yellow it becomes a warmer green and if you add more blue it becomes a cooler green.

Blue (cool) + red (warm) = purple. If you add more yellow it becomes a warmer purple and if you add more blue it becomes a cooler purple.

Red (warm) + yellow (warm) = orange – this is double warm so there is no cool version of it.

The warmer and cooler versions of the colours nestle in between the primary and secondary colours, forming tertiary (level 3) variations. These tertiary variations are the main focus when we are looking at colour analysis.

TASK: Colour Wheel

Foundation level: Follow the instructions below and write in the names of the colours. You could also print out or save a picture of a colour wheel from the internet, but the process of colouring and labelling will help you remember and recall the information later.

Advanced level: Follow the instructions below and use coloured pencils to colour in the diagram so that the colours look like they almost blend from one to the next.

Best practice level: Follow the instructions below using primary red, primary yellow and cyan acrylic paint and colour in each section of the colour wheel. Start with primaries, then secondaries, then tertiaries. Use a plate to mix the colours on. Always start with yellow. Then just add a tiny bit at a time of your other colour until your get the desired hue when mixing the warmer ones.

It's a fact that we don't all see colours in the same way. I accept that my eye is finely tuned and I'm an expert. It's not reasonable for you to expect be the same. However, I also know for sure that it will help your understanding and ability to recognise warm and cool versions of colours if you take the time to complete this task.

The colour wheel instructions

There is an instruction video if you prefer watching: https://www.lisanewportstyle.com/project-fab-the-book/

- Think of it like a clock and start at the P for primary, which is the section between 12 and 1. Colour this in yellow.

- Move around to the next primary (between 4-5 pm). Colour this section blue.

- The final primary section (between 8-9 on the clock) will be red.

- Next, move on to the secondary section (2-3 on the clock). This will be green (a mix of yellow and blue).
- The next secondary section (6-7 on the clock) will be purple (a mix of blue and red).
- The final secondary section (10-11) will be orange (a mix of red and yellow).
- You will now have gaps for the tertiary colours - moving clockwise from the section between 1-2, colour the first gap with a yellowy green.
- The next gap (3-4) will be a bluey green.
- Then you'll have a bluey purple (5-6);
- a reddy purple (7-8);
- and an orangey red (9-10).
- Finish off the wheel with an orangey yellow (11-12).

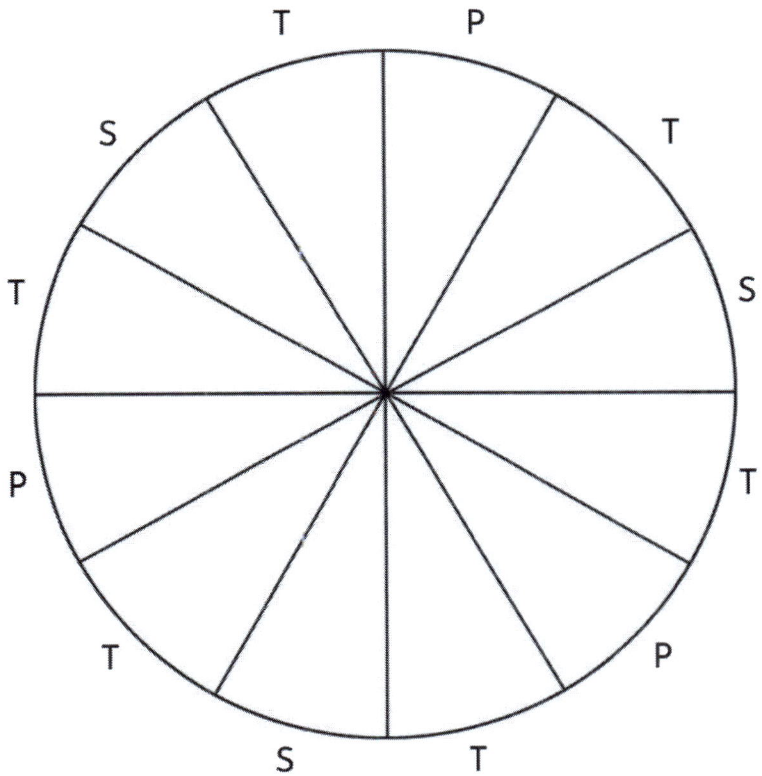
T
P
S
T
T
S
P
T
T
P
S
T

Takeaways

- Recognising warm and cool colours comes with PRACTICE
- Orange is the only colour without a cool version

Colour Analysis Self-Assessment

When doing your colour assessment, the main thing to focus on is your skin undertone. This never changes, although your skin tone may deepen with a tan and fade with age.

The way to decide whether your skin undertone is cool or warm is:

Cool undertones – your skin will be pinkish; your veins will look blueish.

Warm undertones – your skin will be peachy or yellowish, your veins will look greenish.

If you have cool undertones but get a tan you will still have cool undertones – you will have a tanned cool undertone and this may alter the boldness of colours you can get away with. The key thing here is that when you get the colours right for your skin tone the weather won't matter.

When you find you need more make-up, a brighter lipstick or a tan to "get away" with a colour, that suggests it's not one of your best ones to go for.

TASK: Colour Analysis Self-assessment

Foundation level: Make a list of the colours that you wear when you get compliments and compare them to the colour wheel. Are they mostly cool or mostly warm?

Advanced level: Do a visual check with warm versus cool colours. Natural daylight is best, so try sitting with a mirror in front of you while you face a window and see which colours look best. Being make-up free or just wearing a little make-up works best for your self-assessment. Hold up the following colours under your chin: orange versus pink, green v blue and gold v silver. The colours that suit you best will make it seem like your face is being lit from underneath and your eyes will look brighter when you get the colour right. The opposite will happen with colours that aren't in harmony with your skin tone.

Best practice level: Do the "blink test" (see below); check with warm versus cool colours using the list below as your guide. Natural daylight is best, so try sitting with a mirror in front of you while you face a window, and the light is directed onto your face. Use the colours on the checklist below as your guide. You could use clothes you have, scarves, towels, any fabric really – or even pieces of coloured card from the craft shop, scraps of fabric, carrier bags, flannels etc. It doesn't really matter. What you are looking for is harmony with your natural colouring, so being make-up free or wearing just a little make-up works best for your self-assessment.

Here's the checklist of colours for you:

Warm colours versus cool colours

Gold v silver

Orange v pink

Salmon v fuchsia

Terracotta v burgundy

Cream v white

Olive v emerald

Turquoise v royal blue

You want to see if you notice you or the colour first by doing the "blink test". This is done by sitting in front of the mirror. Hold the colour under your chin, close your eyes and then open them quickly. What do you notice first – your face or the colour? If it's the colour, then that's not good. You want to wear the colour, not have the colour wearing you. With the ones that suit you best, you'll notice that your face seems as if it's being lit from underneath and your eyes look brighter. The opposite will happen with colours that aren't in harmony with your skin tone. Work your way through the list of colours and make a note whether you suit mostly the warm colours or cool colours.

Create your list of colours here. Are they cool or warm?

Value Contrast

Value is the technical term for how light or dark a colour is.

As a general guide, you will find that mimicking your natural colouring by harmonising your clothing with your features is most flattering and makes sure the colours don't overpower your face. Look for colours that are in a similar value to your hair, eyes and skin – imagine your numbers on the greyscale below. The darker your hair, the darker colours you can get away with.

Sorry to say this, but black is never going to look great on you if you are fair or have warm undertones unless you really ramp up your make-up.

Once you've decided whether you are warm or cool, the next thing to consider is whether you are dark or light.

This is the Munsell Grayscale. It has black at one end of the spectrum (number 0), white at the other end (number 10) and all the shades of grey in between.

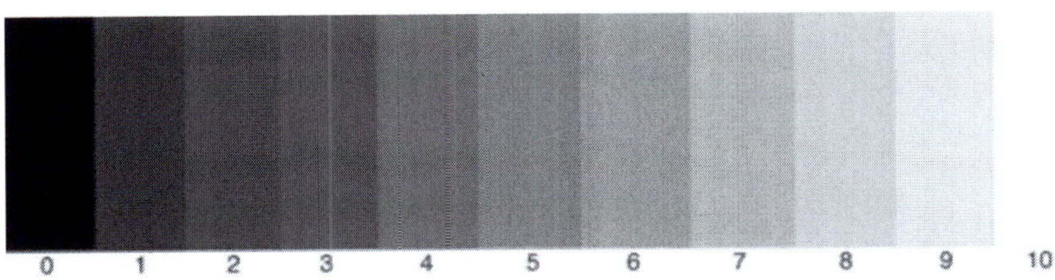

TASK: Value Contrast

Foundation level: Where would you put the depth of your hair colour on this scale? If it's 0-4 you are dark for this assessment; if it's 5-10 you are light.

Advanced level: Take a selfie and put the grayscale filter on it. Check the depth of your hair colour on the Munsell Scale. If it's 0-4 you are dark for this assessment; if it's 5-10 you are light.

Best practice level: Take a selfie and put the grayscale filter on it. Check the depth of your hair, eyes and skin colour on the Munsell Scale and see whether your clothing is at the same or different levels. The most flattering outfits will match the value levels in your hair, eyes and skin.

Watch the video on value contrast at https://www.lisanewportstyle.com/project-fab-the-book/ to see examples of what I mean.

TIP: A powerful way to make the most of harmonising your value contrast is to match your outfits with the value of your hair, e.g. light hair = light outfit, medium hair = medium outfit, dark hair = dark outfit.

Similarly, when you are wearing patterns, choose one with the same value as your hair for the background: light hair = light background, dark hair = dark backgrounds will work well, as will sticking with colours that reflect your level of value. This way you will be the focus, not your clothing.

What Season Am I?

So now you have your self-assessed warm or cool and light or dark value. This is what you would be in seasonal colour analysis terms.

Spring = warm undertones and light value; delicate colouring with little contrast between your features.

Summer = cool undertones and light value; delicate colouring with little contrast between your features.

Autumn = warm undertones and deep value; colouring with contrasting features.

Winter = cool undertones and deep value; colouring with contrasting features.

Circle your season

Spring

Summer

Autumn

Winter

What Colours Suit Me Best?

SPRING	SUMMER	AUTUMN	WINTER
Neutrals	Neutrals	Neutrals	Neutrals
Camel Tan Cream	Charcoal Ivory Navy	Brown Cream Beige	Black White Grey
Interest colours	Interest colours	Interest colours	Interest colours
Apple green Aqua blue Coral Daffodil yellow Emerald green Lavender Periwinkle blue Salmon pink Tangerine orange Tomato red Violet Gold	Baby blue Deep rose Dusky pink Grey green Lemon yellow Mauve Muted turquoise Plum Raspberry red Sky blue Taupe Silver	Aubergine Brick red Bronze Camel Deep teal Khaki Lime green Marine navy Mustard Olive green Orange Gold	Burgundy Cadbury's purple Cobalt blue Icy pink Icy yellow Magenta Navy blue Pine green Shocking pink Silver True red Turquoise

Remember: just because colours suit you doesn't mean you HAVE to wear them. This is about not making do. There's no point looking good if you don't FEEL fab. My wardrobe tends to focus on my favourite colours within my palette – I totally ignore the yellow and green spectrum as I don't like those colours particularly. I focus more on pinks, purples and blues with a bit of grey and black thrown in. It's only in the last few years that I've embraced navy as I associated it with my school uniform.

Takeaways

- If you love a colour, wear it anyway
- Accept that black probably isn't going to suit you

Signature Colours

'Colour is a power which directly influences the soul.'

Wassily Kandinsky

Signature colours are the ones that will really make an impact. These tips are a quick and easy way to get started and a great way of ensuring that the colour choices you make are going to illuminate your hair, skin and eyes and create a lovely vibrant youthfulness for you rather than draining or ageing you. Wear these and the compliments will come flooding in. Your signature colours rely on the principles of basic colour theory and are made up of "enhancers" and "intensifiers" and there are a number of ways you can determine them.

Enhancers

You can enhance your natural colouring by mimicking the colours found in your hair, eyes and skin.

Hair enhancers

Your hair is a great starting place. When you pick out the same or similar colours to your hair to wear, it makes your hair colour stand out.

Look carefully at the highlights, lowlights and different shades within your hair and pick out those colours as your neutrals (unless, of course, you've got it dyed in a unicorn rainbow effect). By using your hair as a guide for neutral colours in your outfits, you will look well put together and polished.

So, brunettes might think about dark browns, from bronze and chestnut through to rich mahogany colours, as alternatives to black. As a warm blonde you might go for cream, beige, came and sand; if you're more platinum blonde then a silvery grey or even white would work. If you're a redhead, think about copper, rust, tan etc. Repeating colours that occur naturally in your hair will really pick out the richness and enhance the colour of it.

Think about using these colours for coats, suits, trousers, shorts, shoes, and boots OR an investment piece like a winter coat or handbag.

TIP: When you wear a pa r of shoes in the same colour as your hair it forms a wonderful "top and tail" effect and creates a visual colour loop that's pleasing to the eye and makes your outfit look well put together.

Eye enhancers

The next step for generating your signature colour palette is to look VERY closely into your eyes. You might think you've got blue eyes but when you look carefully at your eyes in a mirror you will see that there are little flecks of other colours within them; sometimes there's even a darker ring around the iris.

Any colour you wear that matches the colours in your eyes is going to really enhance your eye colour and make it appear more vibrant. My eyes are grey-blue and they always look much bluer when I wear any shade of medium blue through to navy.

Eye enhancers make your eyes "pop" and become stronger and more noticeable in colour. They're great colours to wear when communicating with people at a close distance, whether at business meetings or dates, as they make people want to look you in the eye. They'll work well in suits, jumpers, shirts, jackets, tops, swimwear, scarves, earrings and necklaces. Try them and see the wow effect.

TIP: Choose specs that pick out one of the colours in your eyes.

Skin enhancers

Pick out your seasonal (warm or cool, light or dark) versions of pink, orange and red tints, tones and shades. These colours make your skin glow as they bring out the colour of the blood below the surface and make you look healthier and less pallid.

Spring – coral, salmon pink, tomato red, tangerine

Summer – blush pink, baby pink, plum, raspberry red

Autumn – orange, brick red, rust, deep salmon

Winter – shocking pink, burgundy, magenta, true red

They are great for tops, scarves, necklaces, lipsticks and nail polish as they tone harmoniously with your skin.

TIP: To find your perfect neutral lipstick, stick out your bottom lip in the mirror as if you're really being a sulky, mardy bum and check out that colour. I guarantee if you match it up and wear a top in it, you'll look gorgeous! Also, this is a great way of finding your best colour for blusher.

Intensifiers

Colours are intensified when you choose ones that are opposite on the colour wheel. This principle will really give more depth to your hair and eye colour.

So, for brown hair go for blues; blondes go for purples; redheads, it's all about the greens. Sadly, as grey doesn't appear on the colour wheel it's not possible to apply this tip if you have the glitter highlights.

For intensifying green eyes, try wearing purple; for brown eyes, wear blues; and for blue eyes, intensify with orange/reds.

Think about eye make-up here too. Blue eyes are intensified by browns, corals and golds in eyeshadow colours. Hazel eyes look good with purply shades. Green eyes are intensified by brick reds and copper tones.

Universal Colour: Teal

Find your best teal; it's a great universal colour and suits everybody. It's the perfect mix of a cool colour – blue – with a warm colour – yellow. However, your absolute best way of wearing teal will be to use the depth of your hair colour as your guide to which shade will work best for your colouring.

For example – dark hair works best with a deep, rich darker shade of teal; light hair works best with a paler, more pastel tint; and grey hair works best with a softer, more muted tone of teal.

TASK: Signature Colours

Foundation level: Make a note of your signature colours for your hair, eyes and skin.

Advanced level: Make a note of your signature colours your hair, eyes and skin. Go to your local DIY store and collect some paint colour charts that match up with them to make a collage to refer to.

Best practice level: Make a note of your signature colours for your hair, eyes and skin. Go to your local DIY store and collect some paint colour charts that match up with them to make a collage to refer to. Make a note in your journal of what you already own in your signature colours; make a record of the compliments you receive when you wear them.

My Signature Colours

Enhancers Intensifiers

hair

eyes

skin

Takeaways

- Your natural colouring is all you need to replicate to look good
- Teal suits everybody

Colour Psychology

Different cultures apply different meanings to colours, but I am sharing some of the basic psychology of colour from the western world so you can use it to your advantage.

Honing the language of colour will help you convey the right kind of messages with your clothes.

White

Positives: Pure, immaculate and modern

Negatives: Clinical, uninteresting and bland

Red

Positives: Passionate, energetic and optimistic

Negatives: Opinionated, bold and impertinent

Yellow

Positives: Animated, carefree and vivacious

Negatives: Fickle, skittish and unstable

Orange

Positives: Animated, dynamic and creative

Negatives: Shallow, flighty and volatile

Violet

Positives: Unique, perceptive and serene

Negatives: Juvenile, uninterested and pre-occupied

Brown

Positives: Friendly, welcoming and receptive

Negatives: Mundane, dated and pragmatic

Black

Positives: Dignified, cosmopolitan, mysterious and firm

Negatives: Solemn, antagonistic, arrogant and proud

Blue

Positives: Composed, scrupulous, reliable and dependable

Negatives: Safe, orthodox and exact

Pink

Positives: Nurturing, sympathetic and feminine

Negatives: Trivial, insignificant and weak

Green

Positives: Strong, persistent and reliable

Negatives: Obstinate, resolute and rebellious

Grey

Positives: Reputable, calm and harmonious

Negatives: Unexceptional, adequate and detached

TASK: Psychology of Colour

Foundation level: Make a list of the colours I mention and jot down a few words that you think of when you see them.

Advanced level: Make a list of the colours I mention and jot down a few words that you think of when you see them. Then look at what you are wearing today. What messages are you conveying through your choice of colours?

Best practice: Make a list of the colours I mention and jot down a few words that you think of when you see them. Then look at what you are wearing today. What messages are you conveying through your choice of colours? Make a note in your journal about people you see today, e.g. family, colleagues etc. Note the colours they are wearing and what messages you think they are conveying through their choice of colours.

What do you think when you see these colours?

white

red

yellow

orange

violet

brown

black

blue

pink

green

grey

Takeaways

- There's more to colour than meets the eye
- Choose colour wisely to alter how you are perceived

Rescuing Colours

'The purest and most thoughtful minds are those which love colour the most.'

John Ruskin

So now you know that some colours are going to make your complexion look healthier, more youthful, vibrant and alive and some colours won't, you might be looking at your wardrobe and thinking, 'Oh shit! I've got loads of clothes that are making me look like death warmed up!'

Some of my clients admit to worrying about me telling them that they can't wear certain colours anymore.

So, what happens if you have assessed your colours and realised loads of your clothes in the wardrobe don't suit you?

I understand that you are not necessarily going to want to dump everything off at your nearest Oxfam and end up with an empty wardrobe. Fear not, there are things you can do to rescue those items that are potentially making you look older, tired, sallow and aren't very flattering.

How to Wear Unflattering Colours and Still Look Great

Here are some tips on how to rescue colours that are not your best colours to wear...

- Avoid wearing the colour near your face; keep it to your bottom half.
- Do not wear it in block colours; try patterns instead. Look

for patterned fabrics that are mostly in colours that do suit you – then a bit of what doesn't won't hurt.

- Use the colours that don't suit you in accessories and keep them to around 10-20% of your outfit.
- Use the right coloured jewellery and scarves as an intermediate step between the wrong colour and your face.
- Use make-up – particularly a bold lipstick – to bring the colour back to your face.
- Wear the colour as a layer rather than the focus of your outfit.
- Choose your glasses in the right colours so there is always something on your face that suits you.
- Do not wear a wrong colour on a body part that you want to detract attention from.
- Use scoop or V necklines to keep the colour away from your face.
- Consider wearing a sheer fabric so the colour is not as strong.
- Wear the colour at night-time when the lights are dimmer.
- Make friends with the dye pot!

At the end of the day though, my caveat is always if you love a colour then still wear it, even if it doesn't love you. If it brings you joy, that's all good.

Dyeing Your Clothes

With all dyes, you need to bear basic colour theory in mind. Generally, white or lighter fabrics give a crisper clearer result. Think about the colour of the fabric that you want to dye. For example, if you were using red dye on a yellow top, it could potentially come out orange. You can't use dye to make fabrics lighter, but you can buy a colour remover to lighten the colour if it's too strong. Alternatively, you can soak the garment in a watered-down bleach solution until you get the desired effect, but be aware that bleach can weaken fibres and make holes – you have to decide if it's worth the risk.

You can buy all purpose dyes for any type of fabric, cold water dyes for synthetic fabrics, and there are dyes that you just pop in the washing machine for natural fabrics. However, beware: even natural fabrics are often stitched with synthetic thread, so the stitching might not take the colour. You can end up with interesting contrasts though, so it's worth a punt. You can buy leather or suede dye to use with handbags, shoes and belts etc., and you can use acrylic paint or nail polish on things like jewellery to help ring the changes.

A word of warning around dyeing stuff though – make sure you use the right kind of dye for the job in hand. When I was in my early teens my parents had heard about some kind of shoe warehouse that sold seconds/out of season stock of Clarks shoes. We all piled in the car for a day trip to get new school shoes for my sister, brother and me. (Cue the arguments over who had to sit in the middle or next to my brother, who was always travel sick.)

On arrival, you know how all the weird shoes that no one wants to buy end up in the sales – it was a warehouse full of them! Yes, there were rows and rows of Clarks shoes but definitely NOT any of the kind you'd want to wear as a young teenager. Sadly, my sister and I were convinced by my father that the mustard colour could be dyed dark brown or black to suit the school dress code... We did dye them, but the colour kept peeling off to reveal the bright mustard secret, much to my embarrassment. It was the one and only time we had to make do with school shoes. I don't think my mum could put up with the level of moaning again!

TASK: Rescuing Colours

Foundation level: List the items in your wardrobe that you now realise need rescuing.

Advanced level: List the items in your wardrobe that you now realise need rescuing. Go through your list and make notes on what you need to do to rescue them. Is it adding particular accessories that you already own or need to buy, or is there any dyeing/colour changing you could do?

Best practice level: List the items in your wardrobe that you now realise need rescuing. Go through your list and make notes on what you need to do to rescue them. Is it adding particular accessories that you already own or need to buy, or is there any dyeing/colour changing you could do? Have a wardrobe weeding session and eject anything that is the wrong colour and not worth rescuing. Then take action, based on your rescue list.

Create your list of items for rescuing:

Takeaways

- There's always a solution where colour is concerned
- If you love it, who cares!

I can't possibly finish the section about colour without sharing with you one of my favourite poems.

Warning

When I am an old woman I shall wear purple
With a red hat which doesn't go, and doesn't suit me.
And I shall spend my pension on brandy and summer gloves
And satin sandals, and say we've no money for butter.
I shall sit down on the pavement when I'm tired
And gobble up samples in shops and press alarm bells
And run my stick along the public railings
And make up for the sobriety of my youth.
I shall go out in my slippers in the rain
And pick flowers in other people's gardens
And learn to spit.

You can wear terrible shirts and grow more fat
And eat three pounds of sausages at a go
Or only bread and pickle for a week
And hoard pens and pencils and beermats and things in boxes.

But now we must have clothes that keep us dry
And pay our rent and not swear in the street
And set a good example for the children.
We must have friends to dinner and read the papers.

But maybe I ought to practise a little now?
So people who know me are not too shocked and surprised
When suddenly I am old and start to wear purple.

Jenny Joseph

Express YOURSELF

Shape

Body Matters

'You have been criticising yourself for years and it hasn't worked. Try approving of yourself and see what happens.'

Louise Hay

This element is where you learn about your body type, shape and proportions so you can select styles that work with you rather than against your figure.

When you know about style guidelines, it becomes obvious why that jacket has never looked right on you but looks amazing on your friend Karen. You will be able to quickly and easily filter out those less than confidence building clothes that really aren't doing you any favours.

'It's okay if your figure is slim and hourglass, but when you start to spread and are short anyway, it's much more difficult to look elegant.'

This comment was left on one of my social media posts. And you know what? She's right.

It IS easier to look elegant if you're tall and slim, but tall slim people still get the wardrobe wobbles and I certainly don't discriminate on height or weight when choosing which clients to work with. (For what it's worth, I'm only 5'4" and well up the plus size category myself. Shock horror!)

'I love what you do. I really want to work with you, but I want to lose some weight first.'

I hear this often. My answer is always the same. Why wait?

Let's explore my reasons… if you're happy with your weight, you can skip this bit.

You're feeling down on yourself. Your body shape has changed and things that suited you then don't look as good anymore.

You seem to have lost your waist. You have a muffin top; waistbands are not your friend.

You have a load of clothes in your wardrobe that are too small to be comfortable, so you don't wear them. You can't get rid of them because you are going to slim back into them.

So much money spent on stuff you can't wear, stuff that reminds you every day as you open the wardrobe door how bloody miserable you are with how you look these days. That underlying feeling of dissatisfaction with yourself as you look in the mirror? It's pissing you off.

Then, because you're pissed off, it's easy to fall off the wagon of the latest diet you're on. You try and cheer yourself up with a couple of chocolate digestives or a glass or two of Sauvignon blanc, followed by a few Kettle chips.

It's a vicious circle.

But I'm inviting you to change the script.

I KNOW for sure that you can learn how to dress to make yourself LOOK and FEEL better by following a few tips. Once you implement what you learn in this book, you'll feel better about how you look, and your confidence will soar. How could that impact positively on your life?

Maybe you'll feel happier about having your photo taken – no more shying away from the camera on family holidays, instead capturing those memories of lovely times together.

As a woman in business, that new headshot will raise your profile and you'll feel so much happier being the face of your brand. This in turn makes you feel more confident about getting out there and raising your game, resulting in greater brand awareness and more business.

Perhaps more confidence could help you find the man of your

dreams, as you feel better about putting yourself out there on the dating scene.

It could give you the oomph you need to put in for that promotion at work.

AND… maybe you end up doing a full 360° because you're feeling so good about yourself, you make better choices about self-care – including how you look after your body. Eating nourishing food that makes you feel less sluggish and have more energy becomes a thing. You lose some weight as a result. And you still apply those tips around colour and clothes that you learnt from this book, so it's win-win all round!

You see, it doesn't make sense to wait until you've lost weight. Value yourself now, seize the day, and stop making do.

TASK: Favourite Outfit

Foundation level: Describe your favourite ever outfit that made you feel good when you wore it.

Advanced level: Describe your favourite ever outfit that made you feel good when you wore it and think about why you liked it. What particular qualities did it have in terms of shape, structure, style? Make a note of these qualities and reflect on whether you have anything currently that has similar qualities.

Best practice level: Use your journal to describe your top five favourite ever outfits that made you feel good when you wore them, and think about why you liked them. What particular qualities did they have in terms of shape, structure, style? Make a note of these qualities and reflect on whether you have anything currently that has similar qualities. Are any of these words in your style recipe? Could they be incorporated into it? How could you create an updated version of those outfits for now?

My most favourite ever outfit was...

Takeaways

- Clothes can impact your mood
- If you love it and it makes you feel good, work out why

FFS – Figure Flattering Styling

'Nobody is perfect. I just don't believe in perfection. But I do believe in saying, "This is who I am and look at me not being perfect!" I am proud of that.'

Kate Winslet

Have you ever felt frustrated when you are shopping for clothes and can't seem to find anything that looks right? You try on loads of stuff and end up making do because it's just so hard to find clothes that look nice and make you feel good.

Then you get fed up and end up feeling like crying because you don't like your flat/fat bum, your chunky thighs, flat chest, skinny ankles or your thickening waist. You start wishing you had a different body shape altogether.

The truth is that when you try on things that just don't look right, it is probably because the design of the garment is working against your natural body shape.

It's little wonder that something that looks great on a tall, angular model on the website looks totally different on your 5'3" curvy frame.

In an ideal world we would all be 100% accepting and happy with our body shapes. Sadly, many of us aren't.

This tunic is a symbolic item of clothing for me because it was the turning point of me dressing with intent rather than in tents.

I really liked it. It was a new style for me and I'd never owned anything like it before. I loved the shape of it. I found it flattering; it fitted around my boobs with a gentle flare that skimmed over my belly and was long enough to cover my bum. It was extremely far removed from the "slimming black" baggy tops I'd been hiding away in for a long time as my self-esteem slowly ebbed away.

And it was great with leggings – which were something I'd rediscovered after a 20-year break. (We lived in them at uni in the 80s, but in those days they didn't have Lycra and they went baggy around the knees very quickly.) What seems unbelievable now is that I felt very conspicuous in it at first because of the – what I considered to be then – BOLD pattern. Seriously, I thought this was so in your face!

I'd gained a lot of weight during my pregnancy with my son. Around five stone, to be precise. I felt very conscious of my size, and I started to live in loose-fitting clothes. Lots of black. I hated my body and never felt nice, whatever I wore. I lived in hope that I would lose weight.

For seven years I kept pre-baby clothes in my wardrobe, the idea being they would inspire me to get my act together and lose weight. I yo-yo dieted and lost a significant amount of weight several times but even then, I never got back into those clothes. They languished in the wardrobe and seeing them was a daily reminder of how fat and frumpy I was feeling.

A turning point came in the summer of 2007 when I decided I'd had enough. I remember making the decision that I needed to accept that I was now firmly in the plus size category. I removed the too-small clothes from the wardrobe and made room for new clothes that I liked and that didn't just hang shapelessly on me. And this is where this tunic comes in! It was the start of my love affair with tunic tops and leggings that I'm still rather partial to.

I decided I needed to change. I thought, 'Sod it"' and looked for more colourful things to wear in brighter, bolder patterns. I put my clothes on the diet instead of me and started to wear more fitted stuff, which accentuated my assets and actually made me look slimmer, instead of hiding in baggy clothes.

I get REALLY cross when I hear about other people in my industry who say things like you 'should' wear this if you are 'this shape' or that if you are 'that shape', though! There was one article I saw where the image consultant had written about helping 'ladies correct your figure faults'!! I might have sworn a bit when I saw that. She's the type of woman who gives our industry a bad name.

For me, it's not about faults or flaws but more to do with accepting that we women have hang ups and baggage about our bodies. (There are years of shit from the media to blame for that, but that's another book altogether.) I personally can't go as far as the #BodyPositive campaigners who celebrate being fat, because if there was a pill I could take that would make me a size 14 overnight but still eat and drink whatever I wanted, I'd take it. So, although I don't enjoy having excess fat, I accept that my shape is what it is. I can choose to make changes to my lifestyle to change my weight, or I can choose to dress well for my shape. I choose the latter. It's easier than keeping weight off.

My approach is to give you information, tips and tricks that will help you detract from your flat/fat bum, chunky thighs or thickening waist (insert perceived flaw) so you look and FEEL good in your clothes and become more neutral about said body part. I want you to feel empowered and confident in your clothes, not just aspire to have a smaller waist.

I call this element of my four step Project FAB! framework FFS - which stands for Figure Flattering Styling. I like a good acronym. Along with FFS, I have a couple more favourites...

BS = body shape

WTF = wardrobe that's failing

So, you'll see that for FFS we look at your BS and how you can choose clothes to work for you rather than against you. Therefore, addressing your WTF!

I suppose my main message to you is, really, that in my world we don't have "figure faults" or "body flaws" that "need addressing". We just each have our unique body shape (BS).

We often have hang-ups and baggage that affect how we feel about our BS, and this is when the FFS guidelines come in handy. I can show you how to detract from the bits you don't like and draw attention to your favourite bits, so you feel EMPOWERED and HAPPIER in your clothes. But there are no 'you SHOULD' rules with me.

I simply supply explanations as to why things don't FEEL right, based on the theory of FFS, which will give you insights and enable you to make informed decisions about what you wear.

My ethos is always the same – if you LOVE it, who cares about "rules" anyway?

I'm very happy to walk my walk and talk my talk in this respect. For example, I have short legs with quite full calves. The "rules" say I should avoid ankle straps on my shoes as they will create a horizontal line across my legs and that, in turn, will make my legs appear shorter... Guess how many pair of shoes I have with ankle straps? FIVE!!! I bloody love them.

It was the same when it came to my 50th birthday, my sister's wedding and my own wedding. As an O shape, the last type of dress style I 'should' have been wearing is anything with a nipped-in waist because I don't have one naturally anymore. The thing is, I absolutely ADORE 50s-style dresses with defined waists, sticky-out skirts and net petticoats! Did I care about "rules"? Nah... It was worth investing in corset-style waist-cinching underwear to look the part and feel like a million dollars on all of those occasions...

Sometimes rules are made to be broken.

Body Types and Shapes

In this section I'm going to give you a few tips on how to dress for your body shape so your clothes can bring you joy and give you the feel-good factor.

This is when understanding what shapes and styles of clothing work WITH your body shape can help you look good, feel amazing and boost your confidence. PLUS you can save time and money by making fewer mistakes when you are clothes shopping, so you end up with less stuff languishing at the back of the wardrobe.

It can also be about attracting attention to the areas of your body you like or detracting away from or disguising the bits you don't like. In this respect my work can be compared to that of a magician, using distraction and optical illusions.

Want to appear taller? Wear this length of jacket. Want to minimise your bust? Wear this shape top, etc.

Body Type

When we talk about body types, we could refer to somatotype - this describes our genetic physique.

So, you will be predisposed to being:

- an ectomorph with a lean, angular frame; you might think of yourself as bony.

- a mesomorph with an athletic build; you might think of yourself as solid.

- an endomorph with a softer, rounder frame; you might

think of yourself as curvy.

Apparently, knowing your type in this way is good for fitness training, I hear (NOT my area of expertise, LOL!).

TIP: Angular, straighter bodies suit more structured garments and fabrics; curvy bodies suit softer, more fluid fabrics. Depending on your shape, you might need to think about more structure on one half and softer lines on the other, for example wearing a structured jacket with a softer fabric on your bottom half.

Body Shape

You are probably more used to hearing female body shapes described as pieces of fruit – apple, pear etc. The fruit metaphors are shorthand to describe where our "padding" sits and where we go in and out in relation to our silhouette.

If you remember watching Trinny and Susannah back in the day, or even bought their book *The Body Shape Bible*, you will recall they described body shapes as musical instruments and household objects – vase, lollipop, cello and even the very uncomplimentary brick.

The point of having these categorisations in the style industry is to help our clients to create the appearance of balance and symmetry, which is considered more aesthetically pleasing to our subconscious.

In my framework I use letters to categorise the main body shapes: H, I, O, V, A and X. I think letters are more neutral than fruit or household objects. There seems less stigma attached to them, somehow. When I'm talking about body shape, it's about your silhouette. I'm looking at where your shoulders are in relation to your hips.

Note: these descriptions are based on *looking* at your silhouette, not measuring it with a tape measure, as that can skew the results. I remember watching a makeover programme on TV once where they used a tape measure to figure out a woman's body shape. Based on those measurements, they went on to dress her according to her shape. She looked awful; the clothes did nothing for her. You want to know why?

It's because when we talk about body shape and the styles that suit each shape, we are referring to the silhouette; that is, the body shape when you're looking straight on. It doesn't account for any padding around the front or back, which *would* be included in measurements with a tape measure.

Say you have a round tummy but narrow hips, for example. The inches could show that your hip measurement is bigger than your bust and, technically, using that method you'd fall under the guidelines for a "pear" – or in my world, an A, when in fact you need to follow the guidelines for a "column" – in my terms, H or I.

How to Identify Your Body Shape Using the Letters H/I, O, V, A and X

The best way to assess your body shape is to take a full-length photo of yourself in your underwear or tight-fitting clothes like a vest and leggings. Have your arms straight down but slightly away from your body. Then imagine drawing a vertical line from your shoulders straight down at a 90-degree angle. Notice whether your hips fall on the outside of the line or the inside of the line. That will help you figure out your shape.

Here's a quick guide to the main body shapes and how to tell which you are and the types of styles that work with your body shape.

H/I

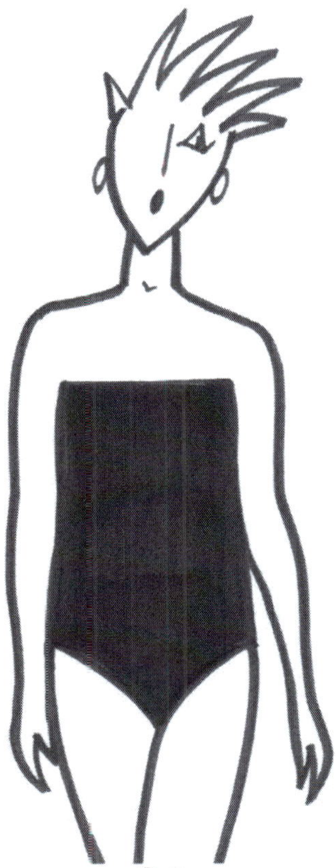

H/I = your shoulders and hips are in line, straight up and down, flat hips and bottom, no incentation at the waist.

Look for shift dresses and cowl necks. Use scarves and necklaces to draw attention upwards. Avoid details at the waist.

O

O = Your hips and shoulders may be in line with a rounded mid-section out of the lines, relatively slim, shapely legs, flat bum

Look for tunics and dresses that flow through the waistline, slim straight trousers, soft fabrics that avoid adding bulk.

V

V = Your shoulders are wider than your hips.

Look for tops with dolman or raglan sleeves, halter necks, peplum hems, bootcut or flared trousers to balance out your bottom half.

A = Narrow shoulders, wider hips; you might need a larger size at the bottom and a smaller one up top.

Look for fitted tops. Try shoulder pads. Jackets and tops need to finish above or below your widest point at hips. Buy jackets to fit your shoulders and leave them open. Bootcut or flared trousers.

X

X = Your shoulders and hips are lined up with a very defined indentation at the waist.

Look for things that are fitted at the waist. Use belts. Choose soft fabrics that follow the shape of your curves.

TASK: Body Type and Shape

Foundation level: Identify your body type as endomorph, ectomorph or mesomorph and body shape as HIOVAX.

Advanced level: Identify your body type as endomorph, ectomorph or mesomorph and body shape as HIOVAX. Consider which styles and outfits you currently own that honour and flatter your shape.

Best practice level: Identify your body type as endomorph, ectomorph or mesomorph and body shape as HIOVAX. Consider which styles and outfits you currently own that honour and flatter your shape. Have a wardrobe weeding session and discard anything that you know is not flattering and doesn't make you feel good. Journal around the kind of things you would like to try that you haven't worn before. Make a wish list of items you'd like to experiment with for next time you are clothes shopping.

My body type is:

✓

Ectomorph - lean & angular ○

Mesomorph - athletic & solid ○

Endomorph - soft & curvy ○

My body shape is:

H I O V A X

Takeaways

- Nobody is 100% happy with their body
- Learning to dress your shape can turn you into a magician

Scale and Proportion

'Big girls need big diamonds.'
Elizabeth Taylor

Scale

Match the scale of your patterns and accessories to your personal body scale and reflect your natural shape in them. So, for curvy body shapes reflect your rounded, soft lines; for more angular body shapes, make the most of straight lines and angles in your clothing.

This optical illusion is a great example of how you can trick the eye. The white circles in the middle are the same size yet appear different.

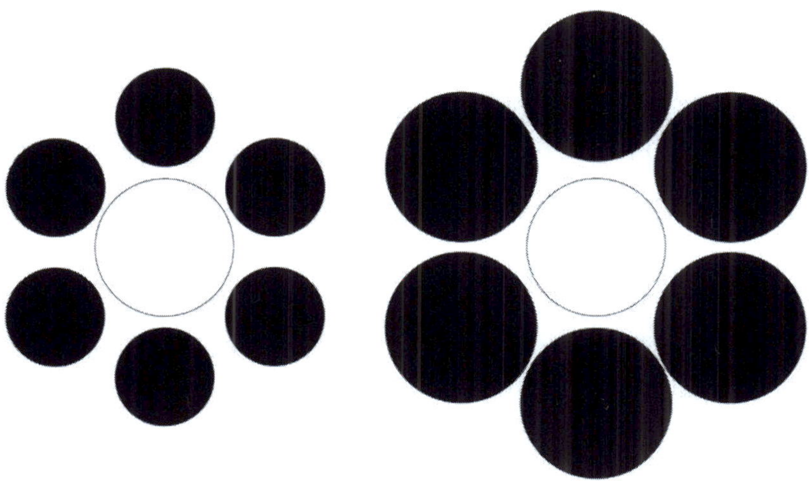

Think about the weight of the fabrics too; keep the lighter weight fabrics for your "best bits". Heavier weight fabrics will help keep any wobbly bits in tow. Texture adds bulk, so be aware that chunky knitwear will make you appear larger.

Proportion

'Fashion is architecture; it's a matter of proportions.'

Coco Chanel

Can you remember your maths teacher's name? The one who taught you about ratio? In this section I will share a simple tip that is based around maths – balance, proportion and ratio...

Knowing your proportions as well as your body shape will help you figure out the kind of clothes that are going to suit you best. You'll be able to make decisions around clothes that make you look balanced and give you a shape that is more aesthetically pleasing. Our brains are hardwired to look for pleasing patterns and balance and that's why sometimes things don't quite look right but we aren't sure why.

Your clothes create lines across your body. Every time there's a horizontal line it's like an underline, drawing attention to that area.

Wearing contrasting blocks of colour in an outfit is a sure-fire way to chop your body up into sections and can make you look shorter. This is fine if you are a tall person, but not so great if you are average height or shorter. To avoid this happening, don't wear a very light top with dark bottoms, for example. The worst possible outfit combination in this instance would be a loose white top that finishes at your widest hip point, wide-legged black cropped trousers and a cropped black jacket, finished off with ankle-strap shoes. This outfit would chop you up horizontally into lots of pieces and make you look really wide and blocky.

You also want to avoid creating those horizontal lines at your other widest points. For example, if you've got chunky calves, avoid wearing boots or having hemlines that finish at the widest point of your calf, as they will draw attention to that area.

The same principle can be applied to tops, tunics and jackets. If you're conscious of your thighs and feel uncomfortable about them, then wearing a top, tunic or jacket that finishes and creates a horizontal line mid-thigh at your widest point is going to draw attention to that area and make it more obvious, especially if it's a highly contrasting colour.

Proportion is all about playing around, creating illusions. Remember, at the end of the day though these guidelines are only relevant if you feel uncomfortable in what you're wearing – and what is right for one person isn't necessarily going to be right for the next. I will never call them rules or say they should be followed.

That said, a 50:50 ratio is not flattering for most people. It can make you look short and dumpy, a bit like an Oompa Loompa. So, I recommend avoiding the 50:50 horizontals where possible.

Check where your tops are finishing because quite often manufacturers make tops that finish for most of us average height women at the 50:50 point when we pull them down. Low-rise and mid-rise waistlines on trousers will elongate your torso and create the illusion of shorter legs too (as well as creating a muffin top if you have any excess flesh around the middle).

You can avoid the 50:50 in several ways:

- One way is to wear a column of colour i.e., the same depth colour top and bottoms. This will create the opposite effect of a light top and dark bottoms and avoid the 50:50 effect.

- Another thing to do is to have a scoop hemline so the sides go up to the hip. The ideal point to have a top finish is the high hip point, where your hip bones start. It's the most flattering point for most people, unless of course you're conscious of your tummy!

- A good way to disguise that is with ruching – running a thread up the sides of your top and then gathering it so it creates a scoop hemline and creates ruching across the bottom section will really help to disguise a rounded tum.

- In terms of horizontal proportions, unequal proportions are good. So, if you're looking at a tunic top with leggings, that would create a 60:40 or the other way around, e.g. high-waisted trousers or skirt with a top.

- A column of colour is also good for creating the illusion of height. This is when you don't chop your body up with horizontal lines. It might be a dress, a jumpsuit or wearing the same colour separates on your top and bottom halves.

- Wearing the same colour tights and shoes as your hemline is another way to add height.

- And, weirdly, three-quarter-length sleeves make you look taller too! (I rarely have a full-length sleeve in any of my outfits.)

When I worked at the prison, as a civilian member of staff, we didn't have to wear uniforms but, as I've already mentioned, there was a strict dress code to adhere to. There was a time when it was rumoured that this might be changing, and we'd be expected to wear uniform. When I heard this, I had such a strong physical reaction in the pit of my stomach. I seriously think I would've handed my notice in. I was already compromising and making do with what I wore to adhere to the dress code. If I'd been made to wear a white shirt tucked into a pair of tapered black trousers for work each day, I would've been so uncomfortable and self-conscious. This would be the least flattering outfit in the world for my O-shaped body and short legs. I'd look like the fat controller from Thomas the Tank Engine! Imagine the knock-on effect of that on my confidence and self-esteem. Thankfully, it never happened.

TASK: Scale and Proportion

Foundation level: Look at what you are currently wearing in terms of scale and proportion. Is it right for you?

Advanced level: Look at what you are currently wearing in terms of scale and proportion. Is it right for you? Think about other items that are currently in your wardrobe and what might be the wrong scale for you or creating unflattering horizontals.

Best practice level: Look at what you are currently wearing in terms of scale and proportion. Is it right for you? Think about other items that are currently in your wardrobe and what might be the wrong scale for you or creating unflattering horizontals. Spend an afternoon trying on things from your wardrobe and take pictures. Assess whether they are right for you and make you feel good in terms of scale and proportion. Journal around your findings.

I'm currently wearing...

The scale and proportion are...

Takeaways

- Horizontal lines chop you up
- Elizabeth Taylor was right – big girls do need big diamonds

Party or Quiet Zone?

'Life is a party. Dress like it.'

Audrey Hepburn

If you don't want to attract attention, you sit quietly in the corner. Making an entrance, drama and noise shouts 'Look at me!' When you apply this theory to clothes, it's just the same. How you wear your clothes is primarily influenced by your style personality (have you done the quiz yet?) but also by your body shape.

Most women have favourite bits and bits they're not so keen on, for whatever reason. It makes sense, then, to keep your least favourite bits in the quiet zone and draw attention to your favourite bits, making a statement with your assets. You can do that with details on your clothing and accessories.

You can control where the party is. My party zones are décolletage, wrists and ankles – so you'll see me wearing scarves/necklaces, V or scoop neck tops, lots of bangles/rings, nail polish and nice shoes.

Tips

- Lighter or brighter fabrics will always draw attention to the area they are worn.
- Darker, matte fabrics absorb light so are good to minimise attention (that's why people think black is slimming).
- Black isn't always slimming – shiny fabric will attract the light and draw attention, so beware of black satin or any other shiny black material.

- Pleats and zips at the front of trousers will attract attention and add volume.
- Pockets are always going to create a party zone unless they are inserted into a side seam.
- Textured fabrics, including patterned tights, will draw attention.
- Straps and details on sandals and shoes catch the eye.
- Ruffles, slogans and necklines on tops = party!
- Fancy sleeves are eye-catching.
- Busy dense pattern is great for camouflaging lumps and bumps.

Be careful that your party zones don't become too cluttered, though. When I was getting married, I was determined to wear contact lenses so my portrait area didn't have too much going on. I don't mind wearing glasses, as a general rule. I'd tried contacts before but didn't get on with them too well, but I was prepared to give them another go in this instance. I knew that I wanted to wear a fascinator and a very dramatic diamante necklace and earrings set that belonged to my mum. I reckoned that my glasses would be just one thing too many going on around my face and spoil the look I wanted to create. I did manage to get sorted with lenses. I have disposable ones now that I sometimes choose to wear when I'm going out. More often than not though, I stick with my specs because I actually quite like the contrast and interest they provide on my face.

TASK: Party or Quiet Zone?

Foundation level: What do you consider to be your party zones and quiet zones? List them.

Advanced level: What do you consider to be your party zones and quiet zones? List them and describe how you can enhance your assets and play down your quiet zones.

Best practice level: What do you consider to be your party zones and quiet zones? List them and describe how you can enhance your assets and play down your quiet zones. Organise your beauty bundles and shop your wardrobe to create areas of focus – party zones and quiet zones.

My party zones are:

My quiet zones are:

Takeaways

- Details draw attention
- Less can be more

Believe

in

YOURSELF

Sustain

Lifestyle Fits

'Fashions fade, style is eternal.'

Yves St Laurent

This element is where you begin to analyse HOW to make your wardrobe work for YOU in a practical way so that the contents are earning their keep.

When you start to look at your lifestyle, there will be no more buying for buying's sake or having loads of nice going-out clothes but nothing that lights you up for work. You'll know where your wardrobe gaps are and shop with focus, so you end up buying fewer items but loving and wearing those that you've got.

Why I Am Against Makeovers

Don't we all love before and after pics? Makeover shows, slimming magazines etc. – we love a dramatic visual "Ta da!" Is it because we are nosy and a little bit voyeuristic, do you think?

Gok Wan reappeared back on the telly in 2020 with his *How to Look Good Naked* show, as did *10 Years Younger In 10 Days*... Both programmes take women who are feeling less than confident in their appearance and give them makeovers.

The transformations are undeniably AMAZING, and the participants are always over the moon with their new look BUT – and here's where I start to get a bit curious – how do these women feel when the adrenalin rush of the excitement has worn off? When there is no hairdresser on hand to bouffe their hair up or make-up artist to give them that full-on face of slap? When Anita from accounts has to go back to her day job and can't totter about in 4" heels, dolled up to the nines in totally impractical clothes for her daily lifestyle? And, with the 10 years younger makeover, when the expensive fillers and Botox wear off… What then?

THIS is my bug bear with the makeover mentality.

(AND why do they ALWAYS put them in sky-high heels and take their glasses off???)

These women (and men) are generally down and feel shit about themselves when they are whisked off into this world of having their styling done for them. There is absolutely no doubt that they get a buzz from it, and you can see from their beaming smiles that they feel fantastic when they see the big reveal.

They go from really flat, rock bottom to dizzy elation – there's got to be a crash, surely?

I don't do makeovers as such. Nor do I have before and after photos of my clients. This is despite the fact that they always look and feel terrific after we've worked together.

It just doesn't feel right to me; it feels a bit exploitative, somehow. That sensational "ta da" thing is private; it's between me, my client and their mirror. I don't disclose my clients' identities either; that, again, is their prerogative. It's entirely up to them if they want to post pictures of their updated look as a result of working with me. Obviously, if they do I'm always really pleased. I also love it if they're happy to write me a review or, even better, feature as one of my case studies. It makes me very happy that someone is willing to share their story and that could inspire someone else to work with me.

This last element of Project FAB! is all about the sustainable transformation, ensuring that any changes you make are able to be lasting and fit with your lifestyle.

Capsule Concept

'Buy less, choose well, make it last.'

Vivienne Westwood

You may have heard the term "capsule wardrobe" and wondered what it's all about. It's about wearing a selection of clothing items that all mix and match and being able to come up with lots of different outfits from a fairly small collection.

You might think it would be restrictive and repetitive and get a bit boring but, carefully chosen and thoughtfully put together, a capsule collection can be game-changing in terms of opening the possibilities within your wardrobe and helping you focus on buying less while wearing more of your existing wardrobe.

It's said that we wear 20% of our wardrobe 80% of the time, sticking with the same things despite our wardrobes being stuffed to the gills with clothes that never see the light of day.

Providing you are open-minded to playing around, this is a fun way to spend an afternoon and as well as giving you lots more ideas on how to wear things, it could potentially save you time and money in the long run.

You don't have to go the whole hog and live forever after only wearing 20 key items that fit in an overnight bag, but you could have a selection of separates in a limited group of colours and a range of accessories grouped by colour that will change up your look in a flash.

When I run my workshops and get to this step, everyone is blown away. I produce a small overnight bag and we play "Clothes Countdown" with the contents. If you ever watch the TV programme *Countdown*, you'll be familiar with the concept. I take one from each line of the template below and we create an outfit! It's crazy to think that there are only 12 items of clothing, yet you can create 72 outfits if you count "jacket on" and "jacket off" ensembles separately.

I share out the items of clothing, shoes and accessories from my bag amongst the delegates and then call them up to see how many combinations of outfits we can make in 10 minutes. The amazement on their faces is an absolute picture. I love it!

In my bag I have:

> 6 tops – purple t-shirt, blue t-shirt, green blouse, purple sparkly top, purple cardigan, pink Bardot top.
>
> 4 bottoms – jeans, pink linen trousers, navy corduroy skirt, purple cotton skirt.
>
> 2 scarves – one multi-coloured small square that inspired the colour palette, and a large silver one that doubles up as a wrap.
>
> 2 necklaces – one is wooden beads in navy, purple, pink and green; the other is silver.
>
> 3 pairs of shoes – pink courts, blue ballet flats, silver gladiator sandals.
>
> 2 bags – slouchy silver faux leather, purple patent leather grab bag.
>
> Jackets – mid-blue denim jacket, navy waterfall cardigan.

Incidentally, I bought all these items in one go from a charity shop for under £50! Charity shop shopping is a great way to experiment and explore with new styles without breaking the bank. When they want to experiment, I often take clients down my local high street and get them kitted out with new things to try.

Shop Your Wardrobe

If you fancy trying to create some capsules, I suggest you shop your wardrobe first. This means playing around with what is already in your wardrobe before you buy anything new. The first step is to try mixing and matching and exploring new combinations, so you create lots of new outfit ideas from stuff you already have.

Step by step guide to shopping your wardrobe to create a couple of capsule collections

- Think about what type of capsule collection(s) you want to create e.g. work/leisure/smart casual.

- Choose a couple of neutral colours plus a couple of other colours to work with. Maybe use some of your signature colours. Stick with a limited colour palette. This is much easier once you've figured out what suits you. These days, my main wardrobe colours are pinks, purples, blues plus black and white. It means that I can mix up my cardis, jackets and accessories to create lots of different combinations of outfits.

- If you're not too sure where to start, use a scarf, necklace, flowers in the garden or a painting or design you like to take ideas from about colours. It really doesn't matter where you get your inspiration for your palette as long as you like the colours – and have them in your wardrobe, of course.

- The next step is to get out the things from your wardrobe that match your chosen colour palette, including accessories.

- A good tip for accessories is to store them by colour

rather than item as it makes pulling an outfit together so much easier. For example, instead of storing all your different coloured belts together, store your red belt, red shoes, red bag, red jewellery and red scarf all in one place.

- You will need more tops than bottoms. Separates make creating capsule wardrobes much easier than incorporating dresses and jumpsuits.

- Now you have a choice of things to play with and try on, start experimenting. See how things look together that you haven't worn as an outfit before.

- Take selfies of the combinations you try and then make notes (mental or in a journal) after your trying-on session about how you felt in each outfit. Maybe give it a score from 1-10.

- Save the selfies in an album on your phone so you don't have to remember them and to keep ideas of what to wear to hand next time you feel like you have nothing to wear.

- Really experiment and play around trying things together in different ways - you might find some great new combinations.

- Set up a Pinterest board and collect styling ideas. Put 'how to style XXXX' (biker boots/pencil skirt/white shirt etc.) in the search bar and see if anything inspires you.

- You might want to invest some time in taking photo of your clothes and uploading them into an app on your phone like Stylebook (stylebookapp.com); that way you can take your wardrobe out shopping with you. This app will pay dividends if you put in the effort initially as it gives you all kinds of style stats - how often you wear something, cost per wear etc.

TIP: Sticking to a colour palette of half a dozen colours that you really love makes this capsule concept a breeze. You can almost pick out your clothes in the dark and know they'll all work together. As I mentioned previously, my wardrobe colours are pinks, purples, blues, teals, greys, black and white and I have lots of multi-coloured scarves that really help bring my outfits together.

TASK: Capsule Concepts

Foundation level: Have a think about how you could fill in the template with clothes from your wardrobe.

Advanced level: Choose a colour palette, use the template as a guide and spend some time experimenting.

Best practice level: Follow the step-by-step guide above.

Capsule template

<table>
<tr><td colspan="3">neutral colours x2</td><td colspan="3">interesting colours x2</td><td colspan="3">level of dressing</td><td colspan="3">time of year</td></tr>
<tr><td colspan="2">tops</td><td colspan="2"></td><td colspan="2"></td><td colspan="2"></td><td colspan="2"></td><td colspan="2"></td></tr>
<tr><td colspan="3">bottoms</td><td colspan="3">bottoms</td><td colspan="3">bottoms</td><td colspan="3">bottoms</td></tr>
<tr><td colspan="3">accessory</td><td colspan="3">accessory</td><td colspan="3">accessory</td><td colspan="3">accessory</td></tr>
<tr><td colspan="4">shoes</td><td colspan="4"></td><td colspan="4"></td></tr>
<tr><td colspan="6">bag</td><td colspan="6"></td></tr>
<tr><td colspan="6">jacket</td><td colspan="6">jacket</td></tr>
</table>

Takeaways

- You don't need tons of clothes to create lots of outfits
- Shop your wardrobe first

Levels of Dressing

'Style is a reflection of your attitude and personality.'

Shawn Ashmore

In this chapter we are going to bring together everything you've learned about your style personality, the colours that suit you and the styles and shapes that flatter and look at how you then dial up and down depending on the occasion, while still sticking with your style recipe. You're still dressing like yourself and expressing who you are but in a way that is right for different situations or environments, so you always have "comfydence".

Everyone will have different levels of requirements to gauge. What might be casual for you could be going out wear for someone else. There are no right and wrong levels; it's all about you working out what is right for you and how many categories you need to do the exercise – you choose your levels and give them a name/number.

Everyone's needs will be different, and the process is about looking at the clothes you wear, your hair styling, make-up usage, accessories etc. and how much you add or take away, depending on the level of dressing you're aiming to achieve.

For the purposes of this exercise, we're going to look at six different levels of dressing that you might have. I'll explain how I apply them to give you an idea of how to get started.

1. Super casual – This might be what you wear around the house, the kind of thing you'd be okay answering the door in. For some it might be pyjamas, or loungewear, or clothes that you've bought specifically for wearing in the house but wouldn't go out in. For me it would be PJ's, fluffy socks and a cardi, no make-up and my hair unstyled, no jewellery apart

from my wedding/engagement/eternity rings and my stack of eight silver bangles/bracelets on my right wrist that I never take off.

2. Casual – For me, this would mean leggings, tunic top and scarf, maybe a cardigan, probably Birkenstocks in summer, and trainers, ballet pumps or biker boots and a casual coat or jacket in cooler weather. I will have done my hair but not bothered about it being too perfect. Make-up wise, it would probably be my basic three-minute make-up – Tropic Beauty boost foundation, a bit of cream blusher, mascara, eyebrows, possibly eyeliner and a bit of lippy if I'm venturing out to the shops. No extra jewellery except for a pair of silver earrings.

3. Smart casual – This, for me, would be the kind of clothes I would wear for working if I was going out to meet a client, going to a networking meeting, speaking at an event etc. I would usually wear a softly structured dress with empire line, V or scoop neck and three-quarter sleeves. I'd have tights or leggings under my dress and flat ballet pumps, boots or low-heeled shoes – quite often wedges, because I find them easier to walk in. I'd add a watch or another bangle/bracelet to my left wrist and some rings on my right hand. I'd have a full face of make-up, which for me takes 12 minutes and involves foundation, powder, blusher, highlighter, contour, eyeshadow, eyeliner, mascara and eyebrows plus lipstick. My hair would be styled nicely too.

4. Workwear – For me this is the same as smart casual; depending on what you do for a living you might wear more business-like attire or even a uniform.

5. Evening out – So for me, this would be how I dress when I go to a pub or a house party – glammed up a bit. In this instance I'd swap my casual leggings for faux leather ones and put on a lower cut V neck top in a fancier fabric such as velvet or chiffon to show a bit of décolletage. I'd still wear low-heeled shoes because I struggle to walk in anything higher than a couple of inches. I'd wear a pair of statement earrings and put contact lenses in, add a few rings and

something on my left wrist. My eye make-up would be more dramatic, and I'd style my hair in more of a funky fashion.

6. Formal – For this level, I'm talking getting properly dolled up – weddings, balls, gala dinners, cruise wear, going to the races etc. This is when people often get freaked out and feel totally out of their comfort zone, but it doesn't have to be that way if you know your recipe and still apply it. It's easy to level up by changing the type of finish on fabrics but you can essentially still wear things you are comfortable in.

TIP: Easy wins for elevating the level are: swapping out basic fabrics for more sumptuous ones such as silk, satin, lace, velvet, brocade, devoré; costume jewellery; accessories such as scarves/wraps/stoles; shoes with a shiny element such as patent leather, satin or embroidery or another embellishment.

TIP: Make-up – don't think you have to wear it if you're not comfortable wearing it or confident applying it. If you decide to get your make-up done by someone else – either a professional or a daughter or friend – then please have a trial first before your special occasion. Badly applied make-up is worse than none. If you feel uncomfortable after your makeover and want to scrub it all off, you'll just feel self-conscious all day and it will stop you from enjoying your event. It's the same with hair – don't get it done in a totally different way than usual when you're the Mother of the Bride without a trial first! If you're wearing a hat or fascinator or some other kind of head gear, take that to the trial with you.

Pie Chart

Now you are aware of the number of levels you might need in a typical week, month or even year, the next step is to imagine getting all your clothes out of your wardrobe and putting them in piles.

You create the piles by categorising your clothes into levels of formality. Start with super casual "wouldn't go out in but would answer the door". At the other end of the scale is your formal posh stuff, usually reserved for a wedding or gala dinner.

Now imagine those piles as a pie chart. If you divided up your life into time spent wearing each category, would the pieces of pie in the chart match? This is a useful exercise to do. It can make you realise why you feel like you have nothing to wear.

I had a client who had a wardrobe full of glitzy gala dinner dresses but struggled with what to wear for networking, which is how she spent most of her time. Her pieces of pie didn't match up but once we'd created her capsule wardrobe of 12 key pieces that she could mix and match, plus a few accessories, she suddenly had 72 outfit combinations to choose from.

TIP: Think about your lifestyle. If you had to work out a pie chart based on how much time you spend in leisure wear/going out clothes/workwear etc., how would it compare to the amount of clothes in your wardrobe dedicated to each activity? Shop for clothes accordingly. If most of your time is spent in smart casual stuff for work but your wardrobe consists of dressy going out clothes, the balance is wrong.

TIP: At the point of purchase, ask yourself if it will go with at least three things in your current wardrobe. If the answer is no, think very hard about buying it. Do you need to buy something else to go with it at the same time?

TASK: Levels of Dressing

Foundation level: Make a note of how many levels of dressing you've worn in the past seven days.

Advanced level: Make a note of your levels of dressing and what you'd wear in each category, then think about how often you'd wear each level over the space of a month.

Best practice level: Make a note of your levels of dressing and what you'd wear for each category. Keep a record in your journal of your level changes over a fortnight and create a pie chart. Then do a wardrobe audit to see if your pie chart actually matches up with the contents of your wardrobe. This insight will help with future planning for clothes shopping.

My levels of dressing over the past 7 days...

Takeaways

- Getting your style recipe right helps you dial up and down easier
- Matching pie charts remove the stress from getting dressed

Wardrobe Characters

"I have loads of clothes ... but I don't seem to have many outfits."

Sound familiar? I hear it a lot.

It's your friend's birthday in a few weeks. She's having a party and you want something new to wear but you're not sure what. You go out shopping without a plan or any ideas in mind of what you might be looking for; you're just browsing. You see a lovely top you like. You can't be bothered trying it on because of the faff of changing rooms and the lighting is always awful anyway... You buy it, thinking you'll return it if it's not right.

You go to the next shop and the same thing happens. This time, you're not sure if the style is right for you, or the colour is a bit different for you; it's a step away from your usual black. You've never worn navy because it reminds you of your school uniform, but you read somewhere that navy suits everybody. And you saw Sandra wearing navy in a photo on Facebook the other week and she looked amazing in it. Her eyes were sparkly and her skin looked fab. In your bag it goes.

The following week you're in Sainsbury's doing the big shop and you have a wander around the clothes section. They have new stock in and there's one of those 25% discount offers. Might as well see what they have... Before you know it, three more tops go in the trolley along with the avocados and Whitley Neill.

The party is fast approaching. You now have five new tops to choose from BUT you're not sure what to wear them with. You've got jeans, but they're too casual for the party. All your trousers are "work" trousers. You don't feel right in skirts. And then there are shoes, jewellery ... and which handbag? And you hadn't even thought about a jacket – it's a bit too cold to go out without one... AAAARGH! It's all so bloody stressful! It's just easier to stay in and watch a box set on Netflix.

This is how you end up with loads of clothes in your wardrobe that don't go together. You go shopping, like something and buy it without thinking about what you already have at home. And you end up with lots of individual items that you like but aren't sure what to wear with.

In this section I'm going to explain how to categorise your wardrobe so you avoid the "nothing to wear" feeling.

Meet the Wardrobe Characters

Every good story has a hero, a villain and some supporting characters. Your wardrobe is the same; you just might not have recognised the players yet. Dividing your wardrobe into the following characters might help you make sense of why yours is crammed full, but you never feel like you've got anything to wear. You could do this in your head by going through the contents and making a mental checklist, or you could do it physically by setting aside some time to do a wardrobe audit.

What is a hero?

A wardrobe hero has enough interest to draw attention and make outfits exciting.

What are the supporting acts?

The supporting acts hold your wardrobe together and help the heroes shine.

What is a villain?

The villains drag you down, are not flattering and are often past their sell-by date.

So, you can see how easy it is to feel in a style rut if your wardrobe consists primarily of villains and/or supporting acts. Also, how tricky it can be if you have a load of heroes without a supporting cast. Your wardrobe can seem very fragmented. Nothing goes with anything else, and you have that "nothing to wear" feeling. Quite often this is why you end up going shopping to buy more stuff to add to the already stuffed wardrobe. Without the balance of heroes and a solid supporting cast, you're on a hiding to nowhere.

Heroes

Think of a hero as being the star of the show. It has enough interest to draw attention and make an outfit exciting. It's best to keep to just one hero per outfit unless you're a totally dramatic or eclectic style personality.

The hero could be a statement piece with built-in interesting details, like a patterned top, a jacket with an unusual hemline or details that create a focal point, a pair of colourful shoes etc. If you are like me and love a pair of coloured shoes, remember to repeat the colour somewhere else in your outfit to create the visual colour loop and not have all the attention on your feet.

It could be jewellery, a pair of statement earrings, a statement necklace (or two) or a stack of bangles, for example. Multiples of layered jewellery are a great way to make a statement. Think Iris Apfel – she's the queen of this!

TIP: If you're using a patterned fabric as your hero, remember about matching your scale to the pattern size. Large frame = large scale pattern, medium frame = medium scale pattern and small frame = small scale pattern.

TIP: Consider the background colour of the pattern too – it's best to match the value contrast of your hair for this. Dark hair = dark background, medium hair = medium background and light hair = light background. This stops the pattern from wearing you rather than you wearing it.

Things to consider when buying a hero

- Is it comfortable?
- Does it suit your style personality?
- Does it mix and match with at least three things you already own?
- Could you create a capsule collection around it?
- Is it a workhorse? Could you dress it up or down?
- Do you have a little stylegasm* when you try it on?

*A stylegasm (yes, that made-up word again) is what happens when you find a garment or outfit that makes you want to twirl around and keep looking at yourself in the mirror when you try it on. You squeal with excitement and can't stop smiling. You look and feel a million dollars and it ticks ALL the boxes.

Supporting Acts

These are the basics in your wardrobe that aren't particularly exciting or even noticeable, but you couldn't really get dressed without them. They hold your wardrobe together and help the heroes shine. They are versatile staples and can be worn in lots of ways with other items.

Things in this category might be:

- Camisole tops
- Plain t-shirts
- Leggings
- Tights
- Jeans
- Basic knitwear – plain cardis or jumpers
- Neutral bottoms – skirts/trousers
- Simple dresses that can be dressed up or down
- Versatile (workhorse) jackets

TIP: Build up your supporting act collection in your signature colours, i.e., replicate the colours within your hair and eyes. That way, your outfits will look well put together.

Workhorses

These are items that are mega versatile: they go with anything, can be dressed up and down and really earn their keep – hence the workhorse label. When it comes to cost per wear, they can often end up paying for themselves ten times over.

Here's how to work out the cost per wear of any item of clothing.

Cost per wear calculator

If you spend £100 on a pair of shoes that you know you'll wear at least three times a week for work all year round, they work out at £1.44 per wear.

£100 / 144 days = £1.44 per wear (assuming you have four weeks' annual leave)

Spend £40 on a pair of party shoes that go with a particular dress, wear them just three times and they work out much more expensive than the £100 ones at £13.33 per wear.

TIP: You can also use the calculation to see whether something is worth buying or not.

Villains

These are the things that you know you should probably get rid of. They might be old and bobbly and are past their sell-by date. It could be the shapeless stuff that drags you down, does nothing for you and is not flattering. Or it could be stuff that you bought on a whim, emergency purchases you've only worn once or just things that you know you'll never wear and could pass on to the charity shop. However, if you've done the wardrobe weeding task, you won't have any of these left.

TIP: Think about getting together with friends and having a swapping session if you have loads of nearly new villains – they could be heroes for them.

~~~

There you have it. Heroes, supporting cast and villains. Hopefully, that's helped you identify where the gaps are and what you should focus on as you work your way towards an all singing, all dancing wardrobe that's fabulous.
~~~

TASK: Wardrobe Characters

Foundation level: Think about what proportion of your wardrobe is each character.

Advanced level: Think about what proportion of your wardrobe is each character and make a list of actions you could take to redress the balance.

Best practice level: Think about what proportion of your wardrobe is each character and make a list of actions you could take to redress the balance. Reflect and journal around why and how you have ended up with the balance as it is. Are you happy with it? If not, what would you do differently?

In % terms my wardrobe is made up of:

% Heroes

% Supporting Cast

% Workhorses

% Villains

Takeaways

- You need a balance of wardrobe characters for a wardrobe that's fabulous
- The cost per wear calculation justifies expensive workhorse purchases

Wardrobe Weeding

This is a process that a lot of people put off because it can be overwhelming, and they are not sure where to start. If this is you, please believe me when say that it will make a massive difference once you have tackled it. You might be committed to your Project FAB! but only have a bit of time to get your wardrobe in order. If that's the case, do it one drawer at a time if you need to. Having a clear out is quite cathartic and you'll feel great once you've done it. Make a promise to yourself to sort it out so that you can really feel the benefit of the stuff you have learned from reading this book so far.

You could even synchronise with a group of friends; it's what we do in my Project FAB! Community. We set a date and check in with each other at set times throughout the day with progress updates and to give each other support. It's much more fun than being buried under a clothes mountain alone.

I call this a Wardrobe Weed. You need to plan in some time to do it. See the different levels of detail you could apply in the F.A.B. tasks.

You will need:

- Plenty of time
- Maybe some treats for when you have a break or have finished
- Bin bags
- Hangers
- Full length mirror
- A ruthless and positive attitude
- Three or four piles keep, sell, and charity and/or throw away

Here are the basic steps. To start with, you should get everything out and sort it into piles:

- Things you wear regularly and love
- Special occasion stuff that you wear once in a blue moon
- Things you never wear

Now put the "wear a lot" and "blue moon" stuff back in the wardrobe. Put the hangers all the same way, facing outwards. Once you've worn something, hang it back the other way, facing inwards. This way you'll be able to see at a glance what stuff you never wear, which is useful for the next time you have a sorting out session.

Hang things in categories and organise by colour so you can see at a glance what you have. So, put all your black trousers together, then blue trousers etc., white shirts, pink tops and so on.

You will probably see recurring themes. The first time I did it, I noticed that I had a penchant for black and white patterned tunics – I owned more than 10 of them!

You may also realise where there are gaps. It might be that you realise a striped blazer or navy cardi is just the thing you need to buy as it would go with so many of your other things.

If you know which styles suit your body shape, the same thing applies. If it doesn't suit you or makes you feel uncomfortable, get rid of it – it serves you no purpose and will just make you feel miserable. Stick it in the "never wear" pile.

With your "never wear" pile, you should check everything is clean, then decide if it is suitable for selling on eBay or giving to a charity shop. (Please don't send dirty items to the charity shops, as some poor volunteer will need to sort through the bag. I speak from experience here.) If you and your friends are of similar sizes, you could even arrange a swishing party where you swap things.

If anything is too embarrassingly tatty to sell on/gift, it is still worth taking it to the charity shop as they can weigh it in for rags. Pop it in a bag labelled "Rags" so they know they don't have to sort through it. Alternatively, you could cut it up and use it for dusters.

It will be worth the effort as you will end up with a more curated selection of clothes to choose from each morning.

TASK: Wardrobe Weed

Foundation level: Have a bit of a tidy up and put everything away nicely folded, on hangers etc. If it needs washing or dry cleaning, get it sorted. Adopt the "hangers back to front" method.

Advanced level: Have a bit of a tidy up and put everything away nicely folded, on hangers etc. If it needs washing or dry cleaning, get it sorted. Get organised and use nice hangers – no wire ones from the dry cleaners. Those suede effect ones are really good for stopping things from slipping around. I prefer those to wooden ones. Adopt the "hangers back to front" method. Colour-code things – all black trousers together, all blue tops, etc., so you can see what you have and where there might be duplicates.

Best practice level: This is full-on wardrobe weeding and it's not for the faint-hearted! You need to crack a few eggs to make an omelette, right? You literally need to get everything out of the wardrobe, drawers, under the bed, from the spare room – EVERYTHING needs to be touched if you're going all in.

Then we get a bit Marie Kondo... Hold each item up and ask yourself the following questions, with a view to creating three or four piles. Get real with the contents – be ruthless.

- Would I still buy this if I saw it now?
- Do I love it?
- Do I wear it? If so, how often?
- Does it fit? Can it be altered to fit? Can I be arsed to sort it, so it fits?

Get rid of anything you can't say a resounding yes to – pop it in the relevant pile.

The piles

1) KEEP – this is stuff you think you wear regularly; stuff you really love and stuff you wear once in a blue moon – posh frocks etc.

2) DONATE – charity, swish or give to friends.

3) RAGS – stuff that is past its best, which can be weighed in by you or a charity or made into dusters.

4) SELL – eBay or car boot, but you MUST commit to doing it quickly – or just put it in the donate pile.

Have a tidy up and put everything away nicely folded, on hangers etc. If it needs washing or dry cleaning, get it sorted. Get organised and use nice hangers – no wire ones from the dry cleaners. Those suede effect ones are really good for stopping things from slipping around. I prefer those to wooden ones. Adopt the "hangers back to front" method. Colour-code things – all black trousers together, all blue tops, etc., so you can see what you have and where there might be duplicates.

When you do this, it will feel SO GOOD afterwards, I promise Make sure you have a treat lined up for when you're done.

I'm committing to...

foundation level ○

advanced level ○

best practice level ○

Wardrobe ✓ Weed

Takeaways

- Be realistic about what is taking up space in your wardrobe
- A clear out is cathartic

Look THE PART

Conclusion

Perhaps you've worked through the book methodically and you're now feeling clearer about your personal style and image. Your intention from now on is no more making do.

Or maybe you've skim read this far and feel inspired to go back through all the sections of the book, step by step. Or is that just how I'd do it?

Either way, information is useless without action.

Being inspired and having good intentions without taking action is like eating a Chinese – it will fill you up for a little while but then you'll be hungry again half an hour later. If you don't take action now, your intentions will fade quite quickly. For this book to have any real value you need to make a shift from being a consumer of information to being a person who's decided that there's no more making do.

The first thing you've got to do is block out time. Make sure you commit to spending more time on yourself and developing your personal style and image confidence. If you don't make this commitment to yourself, you'll end up feeling no better off, and you're still actually making do.

There's no perfect time to start, just as in the same way there's no perfect time to have a baby or for any other big life-changing event. You're not going to be any less busy later on, and you're not going to be any better prepared. Don't be putting stuff off. Life's too short; tomorrow's not guaranteed. So, make a start living your best life and being who you want to be, showing up how you want to be seen from today.

In a Nutshell: Tasks Checklist

Use this checklist to make sure you've completed all the tasks throughout the book.

- ☐ What does your FAB look like?

Section 1 – Style

- ☐ First Impressions
- ☐ Visual Communication
- ☐ Style Personality Quiz
- ☐ Disharmony
- ☐ Style Recipe

Section 2 – Shades

- ☐ Colour Wheel
- ☐ Undertone Self-assessment
- ☐ Value Contrast
- ☐ Signature Colours
- ☐ Psychology of Colour
- ☐ Rescuing Colours

Section 3 – Shape

- ☐ Favourite Outfit

- ☐ Body Type and Shape
- ☐ Scale and Proportion
- ☐ Party and Quiet

Section 4 – Sustain

- ☐ Capsule Concept
- ☐ Levels of Dressing
- ☐ Wardrobe Characters
- ☐ Wardrobe Weeding

What Next?

People who finish this book AND work their way through it will benefit. However, as I mentioned before we can all have wardrobe wobbles – and that includes me. Learning a new skill and staying committed over time takes courage and conviction – which is why some people may choose to work with me. Not only would you have my support and encouragement to keep going, I will be able to give you feedback that will make sense of why something doesn't work much faster than you trying to work it out yourself. Sometimes we cannot see the wood for the trees and having someone who has your back means you will never feel alone.

For those who work with me and join the Project FAB! Community, they not only take their learning about themselves to a deeper level, they develop great bonds with other women on a similar journey and become really great at supporting and being supported.

So now you have the option to:

Continue to be inspired and take action from the book by completing the tasks and working through it yourself at foundation, advanced and best practice levels

or

Join a self-study online programme that will dovetail perfectly with this book

or

Get extra support and guidance by working with me.

If you are thinking of reaching out for some extra support and guidance, there are different ways that you can work with me, and I'm absolutely happy to help. It's what I love doing, whether that's as part of a group programme or a one to one coaching and mentoring package.

So, let's have a chat. I'll ask you some questions about your vision for your personal style and image and work out where you're at now, what your biggest challenges are and where you'd like to be. This will help me get an idea of the best way to help you and which level of working with me is going to be best for you. Together we can come up with a plan for what's going to be your best solution.

This conversation is absolutely free. One of the most important things to know is whether or not we click and could work together. In order for me to help you, you've got to know that you're ready to make the transformation and be ready to invest in yourself. You'll have to be prepared to put in the work. I can only do so much. You need the desire, you need to show up, and you need to follow through and do the work so there's no more making do.

During the initial call, we will get to know each other a little and see whether our personality styles are a good fit. We need to like and trust each other, and there needs to be real rapport. If that's not happening, I might not be the best person to help you.

I need to be sure that what I offer will help you get to where you want to be. If all that works, we can chat about which of my packages will be the best fit for you. Then it's over to you to make the decision about how much you want to invest financially.

So, the next thing to do is for you to book a call with me. You pick a time and a date and answer a few short questions. We'll chat over your answers, and I'll do my best to help you get a clear vision for your Project FAB! and help you feel even more wonderful than you will by doing it on your own. Email hello@lisanewportstyle.com and ask for my calendar link.

Whether you decide to take me up on this offer or not, I sincerely hope this book has done what I promised and has helped you shift your mindset so you no longer waste money on things you won't wear and there's no more making do.

If not now WHEN?

Case Studies

'There came a time when the risk to remain tight in the bud was more painful than the risk it took to blossom.'

Anais Nin

The following case studies are all women I have worked with. You can see photos of these women by visiting my website, where you can also read more client stories.

www.lisanewportstyle.com/client-stories

Sheryl

I first met Sheryl in November 2020. We hit it off and have become business accountability buddies, challenging and supporting each other and sharing the trials and tribulations of being self-employed.

She's become a valued client and is learning from me too! Here are a few words from Sheryl about her journey so far. It's not all been rosy in the garden...

What do you want your clothes to say about you?

Working with Lisa has been a joy and a stretch. I have loved listening to her wisdom and yet it can quickly become overwhelming. I soon realised that I had come to Lisa because I felt like I was constantly making poor choices with my clothes and yet as part of the journey I was having to learn to experiment and play with new ideas. My inner critic was worried that I was making a fool of myself, that I was not learning fast enough and that I was still making poor decisions and therefore wasting my time and money (again!!).

Thanks to the support of the Project FAB! Community, I was able to speak freely about my concerns and felt uplifted as we each explored our own relationship with "our style".

Probably one of the most fascinating questions to be asked by Lisa was "What do you want your clothes to say about you?" I had no idea. But what I did know is that I wanted to say nicer things about myself when I saw myself in photographs.

Style Statement

Becoming consciously aware of my Style Statement, i.e. what I want my clothes to say about me, has given me a firm foundation from which to change how I make decisions relating to clothes.

My Style Statement started out as "Fun, Thoughtful, Comfortable and Organised". It is what I want my clothes to say about me, and it is also what I want other people to say about me.

Fun for me meant quirky, a little bit different or a bit of unusual detail.

Thoughtful was about the outfit looking like it had been put together, not thrown together.

Comfortable was about not fidgeting or fussing with the clothes as well as looking and being physically comfortable. I wanted to come across as comfortable in my own skin and so my clothes had to reflect that too.

Organised was about matching and co-ordinated. I had no idea how much joy it would bring me when my trainers matched the colour of my training top.

Once I had my Style Statement clear I could ask myself questions to evaluate if the item of clothing worked or not. I still made mistakes as I learned how to evaluate the tone and contrast of colours but that was worth it for the feeling I got when it "worked". It is like my heart grows and I smile from ear to ear because I love how I feel and how I look, both in the mirror and in photos.

I avoided the mirror

Which brings me onto the habit I had to break. Over the years I had prioritised comfort and cheap over fun, organised, thoughtful AND co-ordinated. I would usually grab a bargain at the supermarkets and charity shops, the theory being that it hadn't cost me much. But it actually cost me my happiness and confidence, which impacted every area of my life. This resulted in me avoiding the mirror; in fact, it was only when working with Lisa that I became aware that I would look at the mirror but not really look at what I saw. I started to avoid mirrors and so the first time I really got to see myself was in a photo.

The more I worked with Lisa the more confident I got at looking in the mirror and at photos to work out why an outfit worked and why it didn't. Quite often the outfit was fine and it was in fact the camera angle – which led to me being much kinder to myself when I saw the photos.

Lisa is amazing at creating an environment where it is okay for me to be me and she really empowers me to keep learning about what works for me. It is not about learning her rules and doing what I am told; it is about listening to myself and really trusting myself and sticking to my own Style Statement.

Where the fun comes in is when I look at my outfit and know it is wrong but can't work out why. Then Lisa can provide a professional and technical viewpoint that often makes sense of why I was not liking what I was seeing.

Levelling up

The real epiphany was when I discovered I was spending most of my time and money thinking about, planning, choosing and investing in the formal clothes that I was lucky to wear once a year but very little time in the outfits I lived in. My everyday wardrobe consists of sportswear, leggings and tunic tops. Whilst I love a formal dinner party and a good excuse to wear a ball gown, the reality is that most of my time I am in casual clothing and it is when I am most comfortable and confident.

The minute I changed my focus and started to buy sportwear that was fun, thoughtful, co-ordinated and comfortable my world changed. I cannot explain to you just how much joy it brings me.

Learning to purchase sportswear in my colours and my style transformed how I felt about myself in photos and the mirror instantly and this one change, in and of itself, has been worth the investment.

At the time of writing this initial case study I was keen to transfer that learning to my smart and formal wardrobe. However, what I discovered is that was not a good use of my time. In fact, my lifestyle would need to change to justify investing in those kind of clothes. It was such a relief to recognise what works for me and let go of the need to conform to fit in.

Being my own best critic

Learning these skills has really been life-changing. I have just this week let go of a top that Lisa said was my right colour and right style based on her understanding of my style statement. However, when I looked at it in photos and in the mirror, it just didn't do it for me.

Lisa is the expert and so it would have been easy to have made do, but Lisa is keen that we listen to and trust ourselves.

Letting that top go was a turning point. It was the point when I started to understand what I loved and what was right for me, no matter what other people thought.

It is still a work in progress but it is so lovely to look in the wardrobe, run my hands along the clothes, instantly recall how amazing I feel in them and think, 'I really love that item.'

To have clothes that make me smile and bring me so much joy means that rather than being focused on how I look, I can free my mind to really enjoy my life.

Thank you, Lisa, for making creating outfits and getting dressed fun again.

Linzie

The story of when my sister needed my services… In her own words, she describes the transformation she felt having the experience of my "hands on" work.

What's your name and where do you come from?

For those of us who did most of our growing up in the 1980s, this question featured heavily on a Saturday evening as we watched *Blind Date* with "our Cilla". Back then, it was a very easy question for me to answer. 'Hi Cilla, I'm Linzie from Leigh, Lancs.'

Fast forward to 2019, and that question wasn't quite as easy to answer. Let me tell you why.

I was born in 1967 to a working-class family. My mother made all our clothes as they were not a disposable commodity. New clothes were as a direct result of an event – Christmas, Easter and summer holidays. My mum was a dab hand with a sewing machine and knitting machine. We were always very well turned out.

My sister and I were always dressed the same. Often, I had her clothes when she outgrew them. Fortunately for me, I grew a lot taller than my sister and dodged a few outfits as we got older.

When I was given the responsibility of buying my own clothes, I didn't always make the best choices, much to my sister's amusement…

Okay, I had a thing for uniforms. There, I said it. Brownie Guides, Girl Guides and Girls' Brigade. I loved being smartly turned out. I liked looking the same as everyone else. No judgement from my fashion-conscious peers.

It was a natural progression for me to pursue a career in the police. For nearly 30 years I wore police uniform. It was designed for men. I wore men's clothes. No make-up, nail polish or fancy hairstyles were allowed. I was completely de-feminised. When I progressed into a plain clothes department, I wore a suit (another kind of uniform) I felt comfortable and professional in my suit.

In 2016, my life changed. I got married, retired, moved away from my hometown, nursed and lost my mum, and my daughters moved in with their partners…

And 'What's your name and where do you come from?' suddenly felt like a difficult question to answer. 'I'm Linzie from Llanfechell' never really took off.

For the first time in my adult life I didn't have a structure to my day. I lived in the middle of nowhere and only saw my husband

and the dogs. I stopped wearing make-up as it was a waste if nobody saw it. I started living in fleece joggers, tops and wellies. Hair scraped back, as it was too windy to let it down. Most days I didn't care and other days I appalled myself with my slipping standards.

At this stage I knew I needed the transformational services of my sister in her professional capacity. I'd seen the results she'd got with other women and decided it was time to ask for help. I was embarking on a new career path but didn't know how to pitch myself. My experiences were unique and valuable, but my cardigan and Crocs weren't going to sell my products.

Lisa's confident approach was inspiring – it was interesting to see how she worked in style coach mode. I felt totally comfortable opening up my thoughts and wardrobe without feeling judged. We established my style personality and updated my colours – I'd had them done over five years ago. We then progressed to a wardrobe weeding session. It was very liberating: all those clothes that I would "slim into" were about 20 years old. Into the charity bag they went. That took the pressure off. No longer were those clothes reminding me of my failed weight loss attempts.

Lisa has a very keen eye for colour, she has intuition and she instinctively knew what clothes suited me best. She was able to advise on how to accessorise each piece for maximum "wow factor". Her vast experience, together with a friendly, empathetic manner, made our session about much more than just clothes.

Once we had found a few treasured pieces, we were able to style a capsule wardrobe that took the stress out of "what to wear". All the clothes suited my colour and style. It lifted my soul and made me feel like me again, but a better version.

I went from feeling like I had let myself go and apathetic about myself and my appearance to feeling strong, beautiful and more like me again – I am Linzie from Leigh, Lancs again (even though I don't live there anymore)!

Diana

It all started with an online style challenge in the early days of Lisa's Facebook group *Style Sisterhood: Colour, Clothes, Confidence*. I happened to bump into a friend and complimented her on how amazing she looked. She told me her outfit was put together for Colour Contrast Day on the challenge and sent me a link.

I joined in from the next day and it was both fun and fascinating to experiment and reflect on what I had in my wardrobe. Lisa's supportive comments and top tips in the group made me think: 'This is a woman I could work with. She's not a scary fashion dictator; she's a woman who clearly knows her stuff!'

That made me decide I definitely wanted Lisa to do my colour analysis, something I'd hankered after for a long time. That was in 2016 and I've never looked back! I've since done a one-day style workshop, a one-to-one wardrobe weed and a make-up masterclass, plus I've been part of the online groups Lisa runs for further style sussing. I have been a member of her group coaching programme since it began.

Colour analysis was the one thing I'd always really wanted to have and was one of the keys to unlocking my understanding of my style. However, I have to admit that at first, I felt a bit annoyed that my palette was more subtle summer than bright, out there winter!

Having hurtled headlong from my student identity as a die-hard goth – head-to-toe black with high contrast bleached blonde spiky hair – to the other extreme of rediscovering colour and going all out with eye-searing brights, some of the summer colours seemed a bit wishy washy and, frankly, a little alien!

Others, such as pale blues and more subtle pinks, were those that I had previously loved and lost somewhere down the line – along with my confidence in my own style. I recall, soon after the colour analysis, a coat in a pale blue-grey caught my eye and I knew that the "pre-Lisa" me would not have given it a second glance. When I tried it on, I was quite taken aback by how it made me look and feel; it is hard to describe but "shiny" kind of sums it up!

Each step with Lisa has been enlightening, empowering and, in some areas, revelatory. I can name definite "Aha!" moments, particularly in my understanding of style personality and considering different levels of dressing, which made me realise why those "stress purchase" items for a special occasion were never quite right for me and therefore languished in the wardrobe, making me feel guilty about the unworn expenditure.

I think I'd lost my way with my own and other people's "shoulds" for a while too: I "should" wear that kind of thing for XX's wedding/funeral/party, I "should" have my hair longer/wear more X at my age, I "should" dress more like X for work!

I am very tall, with long legs and big feet – more Amazonian in build than the high street tends to cater for – so my purchases in the past were often just making do on some level rather than considered choices. I now know how to choose and wear an "outfit" rather than just a set of clothes and I can dial up or down on my own defined scale of casual to smart to very formal in a way that is uniquely me, not what I think I "should" be.

It was a surprise to discover that though I didn't really think it mattered that much to me, learning about make-up from Lisa, a professional who knows her products and techniques, has an expert colour eye and also understands people, was reassuringly easy and very effective. It allowed me to make a step change in how I use and enjoy make-up every day.

When Lisa helped me to sort my wardrobe, she advised me empathetically and compassionately, beginning with a consultation on my lifestyle and what I thought I wanted to achieve. She supported me in identifying what would be best to keep and helped me to recognise what would be good to let go of. (Some garments I sold, using the money to buy more suitable replacements, some went to Lisa's swish and some to charity shops, and it was satisfying to know that they would be loved by others *and* raise money.) She then showed me ways to put things together that I'd never considered and identified gaps to address in the clothes I had.

I didn't suddenly buy loads of new things; I shopped smartly and carefully over time, first addressing my "work uniform", building on some key things I already had and loved with a better understanding of why! I really began to feel I was finding out how to express the authentic me. I gradually got used to looking for things that ticked *all* my boxes, not just one or two, and everything in my wardrobe began to work for me, not against me!

When I first started to consider working with Lisa, I knew I wanted something to change. I was excited at the prospect of advice and help to give me the shift I wanted, yet I felt a bit nervous about what it might be like to have someone work on my style. I loved how Lisa's expertise, along with her down to earth, honest manner, came across through all her materials online and that is what made me make the leap, though I have to confess that my main reservation was about spending money on myself in a way I probably wouldn't normally have done. I soon saw it was a sound investment in myself and it continues to be so...

A couple of people I spoke to were a bit puzzled, perhaps even sceptical, about the idea of me working with an image consultant because they said I already had my own style. I think there is a misconception that a stylist will turn you into someone you are not (cringeworthy TV makeover programmes and a personal shopper who didn't seem to make it that personal spring to mind!) but the exact opposite is true of working with Lisa. She helped me rediscover the real me, and it is definitely my image, not hers!

For me, working with Lisa has been a journey into rediscovering and expressing myself through what I wear, and I feel so much more comfortable and confident in my own skin. I believe that how I dress is now genuinely and consistently congruent with who I am.

I am continuing to benefit from Lisa's expertise, advice and support and I would recommend anyone who is wavering to take that first step on their own journey. Like me, you'll never look back - apart from to ask yourself why you didn't make that decision sooner!

Adrienne

Before working with Lisa, I felt I didn't look or feel good in my clothes. The process of working with her has been supportive, energising, inclusive and confidence building. She's extremely knowledgeable and inspiring; a real woman offering advice and support to other real women. The videos and workbook are well planned and paced and because they're online you can work through at a time and pace that suits you. Plus, you can revisit them whenever you want. The Facebook group and online forum you get access to are both an excellent idea, as there was a genuine sense of learning together and mutual support.

I feel I own my clothes when I wear them and that I have made good choices from a wardrobe that now is my friend, not my enemy. With that empowerment comes increased self-confidence and self-worth – and more smiles. Ultimately, I realised that I didn't need to a wait for a "magic" day in the future when my body changed/someone opened a clothes shop just for me. I can make informed choices about colours and styles that make me feel better, which means I am complimented more often. But the compliments are just a lovely by-product; the most important thing is I got my mojo back and it feels good to be me again.

It's now much easier to put things together: the colours are more harmonious, I understand how to work around key pieces and I use accessories. Nothing made me feel uncomfortable; being nudged out of my comfort zone towards better choices was a very positive experience. Absolutely no stripping off was required, but there was an honest analysis of my body shape (fully clothed, of course) so I could choose styles that suited me.

There is no expectation that you will be cloned or have your style personality changed to fit a "Lisa" formula; this is about being the best and most confident version of you. It's much easier to choose outfits and I did buy a few new pieces. I also dyed some of my existing clothes into my colour palette and learnt simple techniques to rescue clothes that weren't my best colours. I didn't have to buy anything, but I was keen to try colours I previously never would have worn.

I have re-evaluated my wardrobe, recycling clothes I now understand weren't really me and that's why they didn't make me feel good. I now have more space in my wardrobe, but, more importantly, I haven't wasted money on buying clothes to take home which then hang in my wardrobe for years without being worn!

It is very easy to follow the recommendations made as part of the course, but they are just that – recommendations. You always feel that you are in charge. Now I know how pieces can work in a capsule wardrobe it's much easier to choose outfits. I'm a more discerning shopper, so I know it's better to wait or look in different shops for colours and styles that suit me rather than take a scatter gun approach. Buying lots of things in the vague hope that somehow a large quantity will give me more options just resulted in a wardrobe of barely worn clothes! Shopping is now a more enjoyable and focused process, probably 8 on a scale of 1-10.

As soon as I started the programme, I began to feel better about how I dressed, using clothes that were already lurking in the wardrobe, but styling them in a way that suited me more than before. I have had more compliments from friends and family, despite lockdown and not being able to get out much! Plus, the online community is both complimentary and honest.

I have been completely taken aback with how just wearing the right clothes can make you feel so great. An unintended consequence has also been that I take more care of myself now as well, because I want to be the best version of me I can be.

I started the programme with an open mind that things could only get better. Lisa is such a reassuring people person, who really gets that we are often our own worst critic, and that made me feel safe even though I knew I would have to take some risks, otherwise I would stick in the same place forever. The knowledge I gained on the programme is now part of my life skillset and increasingly comes as second nature to me. Plus, I have the added benefit of lifetime access to the online materials, just in case I forget!

Money spent on acquiring new skills and better knowledge that's changed my attitude to life has been money so well spent. The results will be with me forever.

I'd describe Lisa's programme as an online programme for real women, which supports them to feel fabulous. It's like taking a friendly, stylish, colour expert sister with you on a wardrobe discovery, which leaves you with the confidence to make the best future wardrobe for yourself. I found it a brilliant experience and I would highly recommend it to everyone. Thank you, Lisa. You promised flamingos and certainly delivered!

Jenny

In this case study, Jenny describes how she found the process of working with me on her colour, image and personal style journey.

What type of thing have you done with Lisa?

Online activities such as free Style Challenges and Facebook group membership. Paid-for short courses, face to face work on personal branding including colour analysis, membership of subscription/private groups.

What actually happens?

This depends on what service you go for, but in a nutshell, Lisa asks you questions to find out how you feel about your current wardrobe and what isn't working for you. Together, you'll come to conclusions about what your priorities are and how best to meet these with colour and clothes. If you've asked her to, she'll also fling bits of coloured cloth around your head and alchemically magic up a perfect colour palette for you.

How did you feel before?

Lost. Grey. Sallow. Old. Fat. Unsure of who I was. Long periods of ill-health, combined with ageing, conspired to confuse me, because all the clothes I used to like and looked good in didn't make me look or feel good anymore.

How did you feel during the process?

Nervous, confused, annoyed, angry, disappointed, excited, frustrated, supported, nurtured, studious, joyous, creative, included, spontaneous, giggly, experimental.

How did you feel afterwards?

Empowered, excited, knowledgeable, enthusiastic, enlightened, creative, eclectic, in love with clothes, and a lot more confident

Did you have any reservations about working with Lisa? What made you decide to go ahead and do it anyway?

Cost was a factor, due to my circumstances, but I can honestly say I've saved so much by not wasting money on unsuitable clothes since working with Lisa, not to mention time wasted either dithering about outfits or shopping for the wrong stuff. Plus it's been invaluable in terms of discovering more about "who I am" and has made getting dressed a joy again instead of a chore, and I love "me" again. It's definitely been worth the investment.

Did it make a difference to what you wore in terms of ease of putting things together?

Oh yes! It took some time for me to amass a collection of things because my existing wardrobe was almost completely unsuitable for me, colour-wise, but over time this has become easier. I thought working with a restricted colour palette and garment shapes would make things harder, but it actually makes things so much easier, and much more fun!

Did she get you to try anything that made you feel really uncomfortable?

Yes – wearing camel and brown!

Will I have to strip off?

GOD, NO!!! TBH, I think that would make everyone feel uncomfortable, and there's no place for it in Lisa's work.

Did the clothes sit right with your personality? Comfort factor?

Yes, once I'd got my head around all the different aspects and started consciously assessing everything I had, and wanted to buy, as to whether each thing fitted with my needs/goals. Eventually it became much easier to start collecting the right kinds of things. This was an effort at the beginning (I wrote a sheet of my most important factors and subjected every item to it!) but now it's much more natural and I can choose things with greater ease. I still find myself lusting after unsuitable garments, but I'm much better at talking myself out of it and not buying them now!

Did you have to go out and get loads of new things or could you sort some out to go with, even if they were not perfect?

I was almost exclusively wearing the least-good colours for me, so I struggled initially. I found that picking up experimental things second-hand, from eBay etc., helped me to get a handle on how much I liked a certain colour/style/type of garment/accessory without breaking the bank. I have very little left now from my "original" wardrobe, but this has been years in the making.

Have you cleared out any clothes that you now know why you didn't/couldn't/didn't feel right wearing?

Yes, loads!! Some were hard to get rid of, but once I realised why I wasn't wearing them it was much easier to let go, and in all honesty, I haven't missed any of them since.

How much more room have you got in your wardrobe?

TONS!! I've gone from having clothes all over the house and in multiple rooms, wardrobes and bags to the equivalent of two wardrobes, including all my accessories and bulky items like shoes, coats, sun hats and woollens. This is unheard of!

How easy was it to follow the recommendations afterwards?

It was hard to change my mindset at first, because I had an idea of what clothes I thought I liked and what colours I thought I wanted to wear (and none of those were in my palette), and it was psychologically hard to break free of that. But I'm pretty determined, and I worked hard at trying new things, and once I found a few things that I looked good in it was easier to stick to and build on. Practically it was tricky though, as shops don't sell a lot of my palette at the moment, so in that respect locating things was more difficult.

Have you found it easier to choose your clothes for a day/evening/work/function/holiday?

Yes, thanks to knowing my colour and style; I did a capsule for a holiday and now have plenty of everyday outfits. But I still experience anxiety around special occasions, possibly because I don't get much practice.

How easy is it to find clothes that fit with the colours that work for you now you've been "Lisa'd"?

It's so much easier to choose things that work, and disregard things that don't. I can ignore entire sections of stores and refine my online searches to only show me items with specific criteria. And it seems to become easier the longer you have your palette to identify "right" and "wrong" colours, even if they don't match your swatch exactly. I knew I was "getting it" when this started happening.

On a scale of 1-10. how much did you enjoy shopping before and now after?

This is a tricky one, because I loved shopping before (8-9/10), whereas these days I'm more likely to get frustrated because I can't find things in the exact colour/shape/style/fabric combinations that I want. Plus, I don't need much anymore (!) so I'm less likely to do it. But when I do find something that's totally "me", that's a 10/10!

What difference did it make to you? (immediately/months on)

Immediately I realised why things weren't working for me and that things could be different, which was a boost, even though I knew I had a long journey ahead.

More recently I think I've really settled into my new colours and have really got to know my style personality, and I'm now able to combine things in a way that's a form of creative self-expression, which I'm thoroughly enjoying.

Has anyone else noticed a difference in you/ in your appearance/confidence?

I get a lot of people telling me I'm "looking really well", particularly when I wear a certain shade of green. More recently, I've had people say, 'I really love your style,' which makes me so happy, because I didn't have one for such a long time and was envious of people who did. Now I'm one of those people!

What surprised you?

What colours suit me, especially my signature/wow colours! I don't think they suit my personality at all, but I'm learning to work with my entire palette to create combinations that I like and that I feel reflect my personality. Also, how much changing what I wear has changed how I feel – I'm more comfortable and confident now and have fun with my clothes, which comes through in how I behave.

How best to prepare for a session with Lisa?

Think about what you have most trouble with regarding your wardrobe, and what you want to get out of your session(s). Don't hold back or be embarrassed – the more information Lisa has, the better she can advise. Write down questions you want to ask so you don't feel pressured or forget. If this kind of approach works for you, take notes, start a "style file", begin a colour collage and/or use Pinterest to explore ideas and get inspiration.

What was the single best result of working with Lisa?

Rediscovering my love for clothes and how happy putting outfits together makes me. Discovering the "real me", where clothes are concerned.

What advice do you have for anyone else who is thinking about working with Lisa?

Just. Do. It. I promise you will not regret it. If you're thinking about it, there must be a reason – imagine that clothing-related niggle never bothering you again! Do it now, and fall in love with clothes for the rest of your life.

About the Author

Lisa graduated from Loughborough College of Art with a B.A Hons in textiles and fashion. She then worked as a designer, creating printed fabric for the fashion industry and in the specialist area of the colour forecasting industry, predicting trends.

Her work was distributed in many high street stores, including

Miss Selfridge, Oasis, Burtons, Dorothy Perkins, Marks & Spencer, BHS, Littlewoods, Monsoon and Next, as well as many American brands.

She moved on to teaching others how to design during her time as a college lecturer, followed by a stint in prison education. She is a qualified make-up artist and has featured regularly as a guest on BBC Radio Nottingham and Notts TV.

As founder of the four step Project FAB! framework, she draws on her background in textiles and fashion design and experience as a lecturer to deliver presentations, workshops, consultations and online programmes.

Links

www.lisanewportstyle.com

www.linkedin.com/in/lisa-newport-style

www.facebook.com/lisanewportstyle

www.instagram.com/lisanewportstyle

www.youtube.com/c/LisaNewportStyle

Acknowledgements

I'd like to thank the following people for helping me bring this book to life:

My clients, who put their trust in me and have helped me shape the content over the years – in particular, Sheryl Andrews and Diana Pasek Atkinson for their feedback and ideas after being beta readers, Sarah Fox for being concise and Pam Burrows for asking me "that" question.

My first colour and image mentor, Gail Morgan, and those have met and learned from since – Imogen Lamport, Lyn Bromley and Sue Donnelly.

And my husband, Paul Beney, who is my biggest supporter, always on my side and by my side.

Printed in Great Britain
by Amazon

68382899R00136